Prayer
A Force that Causes Change

Faithful in Prayer

VOLUME THREE

DAVID WILLIAMSON

Trafford
PUBLISHING

 www.trafford.com

North America & international
toll-free: 1 888 232 4444 (USA & Canada)
phone: 250 383 6864 ✦ fax: 812 355 4082

DEDICATION

To my wife, Kathy, your faithful support and encouragement makes newsletters, books and speaking on effective prayer possible. And you make life a great joy!

I love you,
David

TABLE OF CONTENTS

WHY PRAYER?

There is a fundamental question, one that could and should be asked, "Why prayer?" From this question there are several related questions. Why would God design men and women so they can pray? In His grand scheme of things, why does God want us to pray? A full answer to these questions goes well beyond the scope of this book, but it is helpful to explore a few thoughts on the basic question, why prayer.

On the surface, God requesting prayer from His children seems a bit strange. This is the creator of the universe, the One who spoke the universe into existence, asking His creation to pray. To what end is He making this request? Is there a reason why He cannot just continue to speak and cause things to happen? With one word He has changed situations and circumstances, so why ask for prayer? Then there is the Lord of the Harvest, why does He want us to pray for labors. And the Holy Spirit, why does He bother with teaching us to pray? The Father, Son, and Holy Spirit invite us to join with them. It would be much easier and more effective for them to just do things rather than working with and through us, but they have chosen to have us pray. So prayer must be very important.

Prayer is an unusual thing. It is so simple that anyone, even the newest convert can pray. And often the simplicity of a new believer's prayer, with their child like faith, brings remarkable answers. There can also be much more to prayer.

Prayer in some ways is like playing the piano. Given a little time to work at it, I can strike the correct keys to play a simple melody that is recognizable, and as such, I am playing the piano. But anyone who has ever heard a real pianist knows there is a world of difference between my picking at a few keys and playing the piano. Even the student of the piano, someone who has taken lessons for years, while he is much better than me, he is often far from a master. The master can evoke emotion from an audience, changing the piano into an instrument of expression, speaking to our soul and spirit. Prayer is like this; many people pray, some pray regularly, but few are masters of effective prayer. Pray is so powerful and it has a range and depth that few even attempt to explore.

Man is created in God's image; a part of this image is a desire to be expressive. Prayer can be a vehicle of expression. In prayer, we express our longings and desires, our needs and concerns. In prayer we express faith. The prayers of God's children bring delight to the Father. One of the answers to the question, why prayer; is that it is a means of expression of our longings and desires, and seeking answers to right wrongs. Prayer is expression, filled with compassion, and when prayed in faith it brings delight to the Father.

God created us for relationships and this is the second reason for prayer. God desires a close, deep relationship with you and me. He will patiently wait in the prayer closet for us and our prayers. But, He longs to be more than just "the answer man" at our beckoned call; He seeks a relationship with us.

I have a friend, he and his wife at one time had four children all in diapers; (the children were adopted). One evening he came home from work to find his wife in the playpen and the four little ones running around the pen. After helping her get the children feed and into bed, his wife said, "Sit and talk with me, don't say truck-truck or ma-ma, I want fifteen minutes of adult conversation." God loves us as little children and we are always to keep a child-like faith, but He wants a maturing relationship with us and prayer is a key means of building this relationship.

Prayer, more than anything else, is a relationship with the Father. Those who explore the depth and breadth of prayer will do so via relationship with the Father. The good news is; He has made arrangements so a relationship is possible. God has bridged the gulf between sinful man and Himself, by the life, death, and resurrection of Jesus. Man can communicate with his creator; man can have a relationship with God, and a great way to help this relationship develop is prayer.

When I was a little boy my parents would load up our car with everything "necessary" for survival of a little boy on the arduous journey of about two blocks across town, for a stay of a few hours, at Grandma and Grandpa's house. There was no possibility for me to have brothers or sisters as the paraphernalia that was "required" just for me, filled the car completely. Week after week, my dad would load the car and we would go for our weekend visit.

As my parents did have more children, they found that the "necessary" items we "had to have for survival", were fewer than at first they thought. The seven of us could go to our Grandparent's house, on the "spur of a moment" and all the paraphernalia for seven could fit in one car. They matured in their understanding of raising kids and I think my dad got tired of loading and unloading stuff they never used.

God, the Father, purchased the possibility of relationships in prayer, the price was the death of His Son, and though He paid the price, there still remains a cost. We make choices everyday that affect our relationship with the Father. Don't misunderstand me; this is not making us sons or daughters. This growth of relationship is about growth of the breadth and depth of the relationship. I am and always will be married to my wife (and this is a good thing!!! (It is always good to get in bonus points with your wife!)), but our relationship has grown and matured over the years. We are not the kids we were thirty years ago, our relationship has grown. We work at it and we spend time together. The point is, our relationship with our Father should grow and mature as well. Growth in a relationship has a cost, it requires time and effort.

In my example of our family trips to my Grandparent's, we went every week. God is consistently looking for us, not just now and then, but every day, every hour and every moment. Our relationship will grow and mature in direct relationship to the time and effort we spend with Him in prayer. Meeting once in a while, limits relationship. Meeting everyday, every hour, and every moment with Him, can't help but build a relationship.

Relationship is also built on dealing with the baggage. My parents changed from a car full of baggage for one young son, to just a few items for a family of seven. In our relationship with the Father we must also deal with all the baggage. The chorus of an old song says, "Just as I am" and while that has merit, we are not to stay "just as we are". A relationship with a holy God requires holiness. God's command for relationships is "Be ye holy; for I am holy." We are to get rid of everything, all of the baggage, which would keep us from an ever-closer relationship with the Father.

Relationship is built on necessities. My parents found what was necessary for a visit to the Grandparent's house and soon that was all that we took. What is necessary in the growth of your relationship in prayer with the Father? As you find the answer to that question, then everything else is extraneous and limits your relationship. Habits, traditions, and preferences often guide and direct our life; few are necessary, and may hinder the growth of relationships. My parents could have left the other kids at home. The tradition was well established and had been very successful; load the car and take David. However, a relationship demands change to tradition. The author and finisher of your faith, requires changes, how will you respond? Will you do what is necessary for the relationship to grow and mature?

Why prayer? There is much more to explore, but for now, part of the answer is, prayer is for expression, an expression of needs and faith. Prayer is also a key avenue of growth in a relationship with God. The life of prayer, where excess baggage and unnecessary items are being removed, will cause a growth in our relationship with God.

Let us Pray!

The articles appearing in the first unit of this book look at our foundation for faith, the faithfulness of God. Faith is possible because of who God is and what He has done for us. Believing God and His promises is the basis for building faith for effective prayer.

Articles in the second unit explore building a depth of faith. As we grow and mature, God will call us to a greater and greater depth and with this comes increasing responsibilities. To be successful in prayer we must have a depth of faith.

Success in prayer comes from standing faithful and full of faith. The articles of the third unit explore making a stand. This is by faith, drawing a line in the sand and praying until we see Heaven and Earth moved.

Finally, the articles of unit four explore the most exciting part of prayer, changing the seemingly impossible and making it possible.

This book is a series of articles that first appeared in the weekly online newsletter *Voice of Thanksgiving* over the course of several years, so there will be some repetition of ideas and redundancy of Bible verses and other information.

THE FAITHFULNESS OF GOD THE FOUNDATION FOR PRAYER

S everal years ago, I spent a couple of days helping my brother on his farm. I enjoyed the time immensely; it was wonderful to get away from my work and problems for a day. As much fun as it was, I promptly demonstrated how little I know about farming. I will mention two examples, but reserve the others for private laughs at myself whenever I need to deal with my pride. I found out that it is easy to snap a wire fence with a tractor and that it is really, really dumb to continue to turn hay in a rainstorm (you turn it so it will dry!). It only took minutes for me to know I was in a world I knew nothing about. My brother and his wife keep me from major destruction and I, to this day look back fondly to those days, but I know in that world, I was clueless. Many people could make the same statement about the world of faith.

Christianity is a world of faith. If you think you can be a Christian and not walk in faith, you do not understand Christianity. From first to last, every aspect of Christianity is by faith. This includes prayer; we receive answers only by faith.

> *For by grace you have been saved through faith, and that not of yourselves; it is the gift of God, not of works, lest anyone should boast.*
>
> EPHESIANS 2:8-9 (NKJV)

> *But let him ask in faith, with no doubting, for he who doubts is like a wave of the sea driven and tossed by the wind. For let not that man suppose that he will receive anything from the Lord; he is a double-minded man, unstable in all his ways.*
>
> JAMES 1:6-8 (NKJV)

Many religions make prayer, a life of action, if you turn this wheel, if you say these things, if you do this activity, if you do… They make the action the grounds for, in effect, working for the answer to their requests. This is not the way of Christian prayer; Christian prayer is by faith. It is by faith we have access to the Father. It is by faith we know His nature as a good God, desiring to reach out to His children. It is by faith we know He hears us. It is by faith we know He is willing and able to answer prayers. In everything, from first to last, prayer is by faith.

It is easy to forget, prayer is by faith. We live in a world that rejects faith. The world embraces strength, power, science, and other factors of life, but it struggles with faith. Faith is a realm we must learn about, not one that comes naturally. This is almost an erroneous statement, because faith comes naturally to children. They have great faith. They know by faith that mom and dad will provide for their every need. They never once wonder if they will have a meal, because they have great faith in their parents.

However, this faith is taught out of us. We learn the ways of the world. The world's ways are anti-faith. The world teaches that in every realm of life, faith is not the answer and many things are considered more important and more reliable than faith. The more westernized the country, the more "advanced" the country, the stronger the message and the more completely it is received. Faith is seen as something like a fairytale, okay for kids, but something we grow out of, as we mature. At a very young age, people learn the lessons of the world. They come to "know" the message of anti-faith. This teaching is so completely ingrained and so encompassing, that it is hard for those once indoctrinated, to change and live a life of faith.

Prayer is by faith and because it is by faith, just as it was obvious that I did not have a clue to what I was doing on my brother's farm, in the same way most people struggle with prayer. Faith is strange to most people, so they long for any-thing so they do not have to depend on faith. How then can we change this, how can we learn to pray by faith. James gives us a clue. He suggests using the farmer as a guide. His statement is simple, but powerful.

> *Therefore be patient, brethren, until the coming of the Lord. See how the farmer waits for the precious fruit of the earth, waiting patiently for it until it receives the early and latter rain. You also be patient. Establish your hearts, for the coming of the Lord is at hand.*
>
> JAMES 5:7-8 (NKJV)

The same practice as James describes in waiting for the coming of the Lord, is our guide to praying in faith. He states it so simply, "See how the farmer waits for the precious fruit of the earth, waiting patiently for it until it receives the early and latter rain." The farmer waits; this is a powerful statement of faith. The farmer knows he can do many things, but the growth of his crop depends on the Father. The Father must send the rain; He must make the seed yield a crop. The farmer waits for the Father to make precious fruit happen. This happens because the farmer has faith that these things will follow the planting for the seed.

> *And He said, "The kingdom of God is as if a man should scatter seed on the ground, and should sleep by night and rise by day, and the seed should sprout and grow, he himself does not know how.*
>
> MARK 4:26-27 (NKJV)

James' statement is also ironic; the farmer waits. I have never seen people who work harder than farmers. And they work more in the "off season" than the rest of the year. All winter the farmer is working to get ready for spring. His days are filled with building, fixing, planning, and preparing. In prayer, we should be the same. No, I am not talking about working prayer, but working like the farmer. He works with his eyes constantly on the crop; his every action is a step toward having a crop. Nothing he does creates fruit, but without the work of the "off season" and times of waiting, there will be no crop.

Like the good farmer, a prayer warrior, works day-by-day to prepare for effective prayer. From the moment he wakes until the time he goes to sleep, working to remain close to the Father, dealing with hindrances that would cause separation from the

Father. The effective prayer warrior never allows the worldly ways or sin, to bring a disconnection from the Father. This is hard work, but it is very important.

In effective prayer, we walk with the Father, abiding with Him. It is in the abiding that prayer becomes powerful. Prayer is not working, but the work of prayer is to remain in the place of abiding with the Father. The foundation of this abiding with the Father is faith and our faith begins with the faithfulness of the Father. Christians can pray with confidence and faith, because God is faithful. He is a sure foundation for faith. If we stand firm in His faithfulness, we can pray effective, fervent prayers.

> *Now this is the confidence that we have in Him, that if we ask anything according to His will, He hears us. And if we know that He hears us, whatever we ask, we know that we have the petitions that we have asked of Him.*
>
> I JOHN 5:14-15 (NKJV)

To be successful in prayer we need to stand on God's faithfulness. This requires regular refreshing of our memory of His faithfulness. When the problems come and burden us down, when troubles and tribulations try to break us down, we need to restore our confidence in Him, confidence that He has been and will be, faithful for and to us. Take a moment now and whenever difficulties arise, to review and then restore, if needed, that solid base for your faith. We need to breathe deeply of His faithfulness.

> *God is faithful, by whom you were called into the fellowship of His Son, Jesus Christ our Lord.*
>
> I CORINTHIANS 1:9 (NKJV)

He who calls you is faithful, who also will do it.

1 THESSALONIANS 5:24 (NKJV)

Your faithfulness endures to all generations; You established the earth, and it abides.

PSALM 119:90 (NKJV)

Let us hold fast the confession of our hope without wavering, for He who promised is faithful.

HEBREWS 10:23 (NKJV)

But the Lord is faithful, who will establish you and guard you from the evil one.

2 THESSALONIANS 3:3 (NKJV)

Let us Pray!

The articles of this Unit explore the faithfulness of God, the foundation for faith. It is on this firm base that we can build a life of prayer. These articles look at God's faithful nature, and encourage believing that God is who He says He is. They also explore our faithfully walking in faith. Believing in the faithfulness of God, and standing on this faithfulness, we can, by faith, build a successful and powerful life of prayer.

ZEAL IN PRAYER

I like to read and one of my favorite types of book is a biography. The story of a person's life, troubles, and tribulations is interesting and how they overcome problems is exciting. Some people lived quiet lives, scarcely known beyond their immediate circle of family and friends. Others made big splashes on the national or even world stage. One common trait of most people who have overcome problems is their zeal.

Zeal is an eagerness, an ardent interest in, or pursuit of what you want. Synonyms for zeal include; fervor, passion, ardor, spirit, and drive. For centuries zeal was a positive trait. When describing notable men and women, people who had accomplished great things, it was common to use the term zeal. Unfortunately, this has changed, today for many the perception of zeal is fanaticism and mania.

To avoid any reproach, Christians have chosen to shy away from the appearance of zeal. Within many Christian circles zeal is not seen as a positive trait. The world says we must not hold our views too dearly, work to hard, nor be too radical. And too often the Church has agreed to abide by this worldly suggestion. We have left zeal behind; it is no longer seen as a key for success or even as a positive trait. Yet, a church without zeal is merely a social club. Ministry without zeal is just an occupation. Life without zeal is empty and fruitless. With zeal we can have great success. Let me repeat that, with zeal we can have great success. Zeal moves men and mountains. It is the difference between the greeting in Heaven of "Well?" and "Well done!" The Christian centuries are filled with two types of people, those known for their zeal and those unknown. The zealot has written history, filling its pages with exploits. The zealot has changed the course of nations and turned the hearts of men. The zealot has righted wrongs and ended evils.

> *But it is good to be zealous in a good thing always, and not only when I am present with you.*
>
> GALATIANS 4:18 (NKJV)

And what about you, could you be called a zealot? In the things you do, are you along for the ride or are you filled with fervor, passion, ardor, spirit, and drive. The life of prayer should be the life of the zealot. The zealot is defined by Spurgeon this way:

> "If you never have sleepless hours, if you never have weeping eyes, if your hearts never swell as if they would burst, you need not anticipate that you will be called zealous. You do not know the beginning of true zeal, for the foundation of Christian zeal lies in the heart. The heart must be heavy with grief and yet must beat high with holy ardor. The heart must be vehement in desire, panting continually for God's glory, or else we shall

never attain to anything like the zeal which God would have us know."

Charles Haddon Spurgeon

Again, how about you, could you be called a zealot? If you have zeal, you are in great company. Christ was consumed with zeal. The Apostles were filled with zeal. The early church had great zeal. Many ministers and missionaries have had great zeal.

Then His disciples remembered that it was written, "Zeal for Your house has eaten Me up."

JOHN 2:17 (NKJV)

For you remember, brethren, our labor and toil; for laboring night and day, that we might not be a burden to any of you, we preached to you the gospel of God.

1 THESSALONIANS 2:9 (NKJV)

Therefore watch, and remember that for three years I did not cease to warn everyone night and day with tears.

ACTS 20:31 (NKJV)

For observe this very thing, that you sorrowed in a godly manner: What diligence it produced in you, what clearing of yourselves, what indignation, what fear, what vehement desire, what zeal, what vindication! In all things you proved yourselves to be clear in this matter.

2 CORINTHIANS 7:11 (NKJV)

Epaphras, who is one of you, a bondservant of Christ, greets you, always laboring fervently for you in prayers, that you may stand perfect and complete in all the will of God. For I bear him witness that he has a great zeal for you, and those who are in Laodicea, and those in Hierapolis.

COLOSSIANS 4:12-13 (NKJV)

The question must be asked one more time, what about you, are you zealous for the things of God, or merely for the things of man? A call to pray is a noble call from God; the dividing line between success and failure is your zeal. Success in prayer is by faith. Zeal seeks out faith. Zeal will settle for nothing less than a powerful, faith filled, prayer life.

The Holy Spirit is the great teacher of Christians. He comes to teach us the keys to living a fruitful Christian life. Foremost in His lessons He teaches us to pray. His teaching always includes zeal. He never asks you to give part of your heart, he never asks you to care only a little for others, and He never asks you to pray with apathy. The Holy Spirit teaches zealots, the question is, will you be a zealot.

The teaching of the Holy Spirit is training for men and women zealous in prayer. His call is for prayer that is free of indifference and lethargy. He calls for prayer that is zealous for answers from God. He is looking for zeal that will move the hand of God. He is seeking prayer that changes situations, events, thoughts, intents, and actions.

The zealot moves men and mountains. The zealot writes history, filling its pages with exploits. The zealot changes the course of nations and turns the hearts of men. The zealot rights wrongs and ends evils. How about you, are you willing to be a zealot? Are you willing to be zealous in prayer?

Let us Pray!

GIVE US A KING

And God said to Noah… "Make yourself an ark of gopherwood". We read this and jump to, "thus Noah did", but we do not think about how strange this must have seemed to the people of that time. You can just imagine some of the conversations, "Did you hear, some old man is building a big boat or something", "He is going to put the animals in this boat he is building." This was a part of God's master plan for the salvation of mankind and a wonderful picture of salvation through our redeemer, Jesus Christ. However, wonderful as it was, and is, it had to be on everyone's list of strange things.

People do strange things at times. Everyone can relate to the strange things people do, because we have all, been there and done that. An example of doing strange things is a choice the Jews made. They had a good thing going; they were God's chosen people. I think we would all agree that was a good thing. However, they did something strange; the Jews told God they did not want to be a special people any more. They asked to be just like other nations.

But the thing displeased Samuel when they said, "Give us a king to judge us." So Samuel prayed to the Lord. And the Lord said to Samuel, Heed the voice of the people in all that they say to you; for they have not rejected you, but they have rejected Me, that I should not reign over them.

I SAMUEL 8:6-7 (NKJV)

Strange as this seems at first it is understandable; they were required to do things God's way because they were His people. They thought if they were like other nations, with a king, they would not have to follow God's requirements. This was kind of like the idea that the grass is always greener on the other side of the fence. "Gentile people are all rich, live well, and are not under all these rules", was the view from the Jewish side of the fence. The reality was far different, but often people see what they want to see.

The Jewish people pressed Samuel. He explained how difficult it would be to have a king, He told them what a burden having a king was, still the people cried for a king. They were thinking, if we have a king, he will lead us and we will be like other people; life will be better and much easier. Surely it is easier to have a king, than it is to follow all of God's rules. Even though God's leading was much better than anything an earthly king could do, the people chose a king over following God. They chose a king so they could live as they wanted. So God gave them King Saul.

Now therefore, heed their voice. However, you shall solemnly forewarn them, and show them the behavior of the king who will reign over them.

I SAMUEL 8:9 (NKJV)

Things do not change; people are people and make strange choices. Often they see things as though they were looking through tinted glasses. They want to do things their way instead of following God's way. Just as the Jews demanded a king, so people make demands today. People think things would be better if they did not have to follow God. They long to be free as they view people of the world. The illusion is not accurate, living in the world does not make us free, but the illusion is so strong many people choose to go that way. Unfortunately, with this illusion, many Christians want to be just like non-Christians.

Christians have great promises from God; He has promised to help, defend, provide, and deliver. He has promised to do more than we can imagine. However, even with all these wonderful promises from God, too often, Christians think it would be easier or better to be just like the world. The illusion of the so called good life, clouds vision and brings the poor choice of seeking the world.

It may be foolishness, but often Christians try to act like the world, talk like the world, and sin like the world. They try to be just like the world and not be different. At the same time, these same Christians recognize that there are benefits with being a Christian, so they still want God to help, defend, provide, deliver, and so forth. They want the good things of the Christian life, but without any of God's rules and regulations, without any burden or demands.

When we choose to walk as the world, following its ways and means, we make the power of God limited or of no effect in our life and church. The demise of Christianity in many areas today is a direct result of the exclusion of God and His power. The Christian church without God and His power is nothing more than a social club.

Some social clubs do very good things; however, the church can and should be so much more. The Church has been called to preach the Gospel. That is to tell the world and demonstrate to the world, the good news of salvation in Christ Jesus. This is good news for all who will hear and the most important thing needed by the world and the number one job of the Church.

Seeking to be like the world restricts what we can do. Why would we want to limit ourselves? Most often the reason is our desire to be like the world? Why do we make these poor choices and hurt ourselves? There are many reasons, but the bottom line is we are still rebelling against God. We try to let the flesh rule, seeking pleasure in the things of the world. We want to run our lives and do things our way. We want to have it all, the illusion and God. We want to have God supply our every wish and need, but under our control, as we direct, and without interference and restriction. We want God to be our slave.

Each of us must examine ourselves and check out our life, works, and words. What do they say about me? Do they declare my continued longing and efforts to live in the world? How much of the world's ways are my ways? Do I daily long for the things of the world or for the Kingdom of God?

> *if My people who are called by My name will humble themselves, and pray and seek My face, and turn from their wicked ways, then I will hear from heaven, and will forgive their sin and heal their land.*
>
> 2 CHRONICLES 7:14 (NKJV)

If we are going to be effective in prayer we must pray in faith. To do so we must begin by first and foremost seeking God as King in our life. God answers prayer and this is the best thing that could happen to us. However, we must come to Him on His terms. We cannot effectively pray if we are seeking the world and its ways at the same time claiming to be seeking His ways, His blessings, and His answers. Placing God as King over our life opens doors for answers to prayer. When He is King, then our life, work, and prayers should be and will be, our top priority.

> *But seek first the kingdom of God and His righteousness,*
> *and all these things shall be added to you.*
>
> MATTHEW 6:33 (NKJV)

Faith filled prayers begin with faithfulness to God and seeking Him and the advance of His kingdom. He has called us to have a part in what He is doing; He has called us to pray and has promised to answer our prayers. To be effective in prayer we must seek to make God, and God alone, King over our life. Those with eyes to see and ears to hear; know they can only have one King. He is the true King, He is God. The wise man seeks to follow Him and Him alone. "We Will Have No King, but God."

Let us Pray!

WAVER NOT

People who are serious about prayer are looking for answers to their prayers. They want an abundance of answers, timely answers, and powerful answers to prayer. In the Bible, James explains what we want; prayers that avail much (James 5:16). The question is how can we make progress toward this goal? To make progress in prayer, it must be by faith. Faith believes the promises of God. Unfortunately, most people waver on this. They doubt God and so they are tossed about and fail to have the success in prayer they desire.

> *But let him ask in faith, with no doubting, for he who doubts is like a wave of the sea driven and tossed by the wind.*
>
> JAMES 1:6 (NKJV)

Prayer is the mightiest force on earth; it moves mountains and changes the path of nations. Powerful prayer begins with God; there is no other source of this power. God's promises concerning prayer, describe an unlimited power supply available to all who will pray, that is to all who will pray following God's directions and commands.

The power of prayer is great. We are at a junction of time where we need answers to prayer; we must have answers to prayer. However, we see few answers. God is not the problem with our lack of powerful prayer and answers. He is every day the same, the power that created the universe is still His and at His command. The problem is with us. There are many areas where we fail to meet our part in prayer.

As mentioned before, too often we have wavered at the promises of God through unbelief. We do not stand firm in our belief that God can do what He says He can do. We let our views and ideas, and the views and ideas of the world, dictate what we believe. Too often we are like the people who lived in the area around Jesus' home. Unbelief kept them from seeing great miracles.

> *Now He did not do many mighty works there because of their unbelief.*
>
> MATTHEW 13:58 (NKJV)

The same is true today; we do not see the mighty works of God because too often there is unbelief in our prayers. By way of contrast look at the example of Abraham, he was a man just like us, but he did not waver at the promises of God through unbelief. He was fully convinced that what God promised, God was able to do.

> *He did not waver at the promise of God through unbelief, but was strengthened in faith, giving glory to God, and being fully convinced that what He had promised He was also able to perform. And therefore "it was accounted to him for righteousness".*
>
> ROMANS 4:20-22 (NKJV)

So what are we to do? The answer is, follow the example of Abraham. Notice what he did to strengthen his faith, he gave glory to God. We can do the same thing, as Abraham. We can and must strengthen our faith, and we do this by giving glory to God, and by being fully convinced of his promise keeping nature.

Faith comes by hearing the Word of God. To strengthen our faith we need to immerse ourselves in the Word of God. This is not just reading, but total engagement in the Word. We need to focus on the scriptures about faith and the promises of God. What has God said He will do? What is His record of doing what He has said? Too many people are satisfied with reading the promises once and passing on, but this does not strengthen their faith. Immersion is the key to success here. Read the Bible, listen to scriptures and faith filled teaching, memorize key verses on faith, study passages on faith, and meditate on the Word of God and especially on His promises.

If we are going to put an end to wavering at the promises of God, we need to be like Abraham, we need to be fully convinced. To be convinced means you have overpowered all arguments. For Abraham and for us, this is overcoming all arguments contrary to the promises of God. God's Word overcomes doubt, fear, reservations, misgivings, distrust, disbelief, qualms, suspicions, skepticisms, hesitation, and uncertainty concerning God and His promises. As we study God's Word we should come to the point of being fully convinced.

> *by which have been given to us exceedingly great and*
> *precious promises, that through these you may be partakers*
> *of the divine nature, having escaped the corruption that is*
> *in the world through lust.*
>
> 2 PETER 1:4 (NKJV)

Exceedingly great and precious promises, this is high praise and well deserved, for these promises of God. It is important if we are going to progress in our prayer life, that we come to more fully recognize the promises of God for what they are and what they mean for us. God's promises are directly related to the answers we seek and need in prayer. Answers to prayer are the fulfillment of God's promises. When Paul states that God will do exceedingly, abundantly more than we can ask (see Ephesians 3:20) He is telling us that God's promises are the answers to prayer that we are asking for and they are so much more.

The word translated as promise in this verse (2 Peter 1:4), means; a self-committal assurance of conferring some good. Peter is telling us that God has committed Himself to bestow good on us. The promises of God are His commitment to you and to me, a commitment that He will do good things. God has committed Himself!

It is great, we can have confidence in God and His promises, and there is still more. Not only does He keep His promises and He has exceeding great power. His promises are life changing, yoke destroying, mountain moving, and covenant fulfilling power. He is able to do exceedingly, abundantly above all that we ask or think. And we can have confidence in God and His power to bring the fulfillment of His promises. He is able, willing, and faithful to do what He promises.

the eyes of your understanding being enlightened; that
you may know what is the hope of His calling, what are
the riches of the glory of His inheritance in the saints,
and what is the exceeding greatness of His power toward

us who believe, according to the working of His mighty power

EPHESIANS 1:18-19 (NKJV)

Let us hold fast the confession of our hope without wavering, for He who promised is faithful.

HEBREWS 10:23 (NKJV)

For you have need of endurance, so that after you have done the will of God, you may receive the promise:

HEBREWS 10:36 (NKJV)

For effective prayer we must come to the point where we do not waver at the promises of God. Meditate on the promises of God as you read and study the Bible, look for the promises of God and make note of these great promises. Invite the Holy Spirit to show you promises that deal with an area for which you are actively seeking God's answer. Confess this promise, let nothing cross your lips that would deny, reject, modify, or counter your belief that God is faithful to His promise and able to do what He has said He would do. Act on His promise and do not let anything keep you from seeing His promise fulfilled.

Let us Pray!

THE REFRESHING PROMISES

One summer while working with a missions team, a group of us went to the beach along the coast of Wales for a picnic. We had a grand time and on the way back to our cars, we crossed a large expanse of beach that had been mostly covered with water when we had walked to our picnic location. On this return trip the tide was out and we found a spring bubbling up clear cold water. This had been completely covered before, but now we could see the water. Our host suggested that the water was fresh and clean enough to drink so we tried it. The water tasted wonderful and was very refreshing. Sometimes in our daily walk we need times like this, times of refreshing. The promises of God should be like this for us; they are refreshing for all who remember them and hold on to them.

Having times of refreshing is important. In the Christian life and in the life of prayer, we face tough periods at times. The nature of the world we live in and the efforts of the Devil, work against us. This makes for times when we struggle with our faith. There is nothing wrong with God's side of faith. He has made provision for us. Jesus is the author and finisher of our faith.

> *looking unto Jesus, the author and finisher of our faith,*
> *who for the joy that was set before Him endured the cross,*
> *despising the shame, and has sat down at the right hand*
> *of the throne of God.*
>
> HEBREWS 12:2 (NKJV)

Jesus' work has not changed, He authors, that is starts our faith and He completes our faith. The problem in our daily walk of faith is the area of the "and". Between the start of our faith and the finish of our faith is that time when we can grow weary. This is usually when the Devil attacks. He works to make us weary and loose sight of the great and precious promises of God. Then he works with unbelief, trying to make our faith fail.

The Old Testament records times when the Jewish people lost sight of the promises of God and their faith failed. A great example is the return of the spies who had gone to scout out the Promised Land. This land was called the Promised Land because God had promised the Jewish people a special place, a land that flowed with milk and honey. He had promised to take them there. This was a great promise of God. Caleb and Joshua had their eyes on the promise of God. They were ready to go and take the land. They were ready to stand firm in faith believing that if God promised He could and would do what He promised.

> *Then Caleb quieted the people before Moses, and said,*
> *"Let us go up at once and take possession, for we are well*
> *able to overcome it."*
>
> NUMBERS 13:30 (NKJV)

24

Unfortunately the other spies and the people did not keep their eyes on the promise. They saw the problems and hindrances that would defeat them, not the promises of God. Their faith failed. The question today is what about us. Will we be like Caleb and Joshua and keep our eyes on the promises of God or will we be like the other people. It is relatively easy to say we will be like Caleb and Joshua, especially when we are with God, such as in church or a time of worship. However, the problem is when we are in the tough times. When we are facing the issues of life and the problems thrown at us that are intended to kill, steal, and destroy our life and faith.

> *Therefore, since a promise remains of entering His rest, let us fear lest any of you seem to have come short of it. For indeed the gospel was preached to us as well as to them; but the word which they heard did not profit them, not being mixed with faith in those who heard it.*
> HEBREWS 4:1-2 (NKJV)

> *Let us therefore be diligent to enter that rest, lest anyone fall according to the same example of disobedience.*
> HEBREWS 4:11 (NKJV)

We can be like Caleb and Joshua and take the land. We can patiently endure the hard times and with the promises of God we are well able to overcome any obstacle the Devil can throw at us. Caleb saw the Promised Land and the promise of God and He was fully persuaded that God was able to go before them and take the land. We must be like Caleb and have our eyes on the promises of God. What has God promised you concerning your prayers? What has He said He would do? Then keep your eyes on Him and see Him do the great and mighty things He has promised.

After all the people except for Caleb and Joshua had died in the desert, God did just what He had promised He gave them the Promised Land. Caleb was right; God could and would do what He said. Although he was much older, he never took his eyes off the promise and he saw God's promise fulfilled. We can and should do the same. God has promised, so we should and can walk with Him, keeping our eyes on Him and His promises. If we do, we will see Him do great things for us. And that is refreshing!

Let us Pray!

ARTICLE 5

THE MILLIONAIRE

When I was a little boy there was a TV show we watched called the Millionaire. Each week Mr. Malone would deliver a check to a person. The check was for one million, tax free, dollars, a lot of money especially in those days. The program was based on following what would happen to the recipient of the money. The show was popular because you did not know how it would turn out. Some weeks the money caused a good turn-around in the person's life. There was some form of the rags-to-riches story and it was a feel-good show. Other weeks the money would destroy the person's life. Hatred, anger, jealousy, pettiness, and other evils, would dominate the person or those around them and the result was bad. Nearly all of the people visited by Mr. Malone were unprepared for his visit and the money. They had to scramble to decide what they would do. Some made good choices and others made poor choices.

What would you do if Mr. Malone came to your door today? In the TV show he brought one million dollars, but adjusted for inflation, now he is bringing 10 or 20 million. If he came and said, "Here is a check from an anonymous donor." What would you do? Would you pay off the mortgage on your house? Pay for your cars? Give money to family members? Would you be able to handle this sudden wealth or would evil desires overwhelm you and cause you to fall into problems?

There is one standing at your door, He is far greater than the anonymous donor who sent Mr. Malone. He is knocking at your door. He comes with His great and precious promises. These promises are His pledge to do more than we can ask or imagine. These promises are a commitment to answer our prayers. These promises are backed by God who states that all the silver and gold is His. These promises are assurance of supplying for our every need. These are great promises, far better than any check Mr. Malone could bring. And to make this even better, the blessing of God comes without sorrow.

> *The blessing of the Lord makes one rich, And He adds no sorrow with it.*
>
> PROVERBS 10:22 (NKJV)

So what would you do if God sent a Mr. Malone to you today? Are you prepared to receive from Him? Naturally we would answer yes, I am ready. But are we? What would happen to you if you suddenly had millions of dollars? Would you still walk your Christian life? Would you give to the poor or hoard to yourself? Would you live hidden away so no one could steal from you, hiding away from all those people and problems? Are there things in your heart that would rise up and make life with you a living hell? This is what happened on some episodes of the TV show. So the question is, are you ready? Are you prepared?

> *But in a great house there are not only vessels of gold and silver, but also of wood and clay, some for honor and some for dishonor. Therefore if anyone cleanses himself from*

the latter, he will be a vessel for honor, sanctified and useful for the Master, prepared for every good work. Flee also youthful lusts; but pursue righteousness, faith, love, peace with those who call on the Lord out of a pure heart. But avoid foolish and ignorant disputes, knowing that they generate strife.

2 TIMOTHY 2:20-23 (NKJV)

The next question is; what promise has God made to you? People enjoyed the TV show. It was popular, but people saw it as presenting unreal situations because they claimed that nothing like that ever happened to real people. The same is said by many concerning the promises of God. Those people in the Bible had those promises, but not me.

The promises of God remain, but they are waiting for someone to answer the door and receive them. He is knocking, are you going to the door? God has not changed, He is the same yesterday, today, and forever and His promises are available to us today, for the meeting of needs around us. He is waiting, but few people even come to the door. Will you claim His promises and let Him work in your life and in your prayers?

Finally, you have a ministry in prayer. You are called to pray for your government and nation (to allow living in peace and for the spreading of the Gospel), to pray for the needs of people around you, to pray for the success of your church, and much more. You are called to pray. Your prayers can be a practice of frustration, where nothing happens or you can pray effective, fervent prayers that avail much.

Effective prayers must be prayers, prayed in faith. Without faith nothing will happen. Will you be one of those people who believe the promises of God? Will you be a man or woman of faith who without wavering, without unbelief, being strong in faith, believes the promises of God?

He did not waver at the promise of God through unbelief, but was strengthened in faith, giving glory to God, and being fully convinced that what He had promised He was also able to perform.

ROMANS 4:20-21 (NKJV)

by which have been given to us exceedingly great and precious promises, that through these you may be partakers of the divine nature, having escaped the corruption that is in the world through lust.

2 PETER 1:4 (NKJV)

We need to have specific promises from God. Promises we hold tightly to, believing that God will faithfully do what He has promised. These promises are ours for the taking and they must be ours by faith. God is looking for men and women who will believe Him. Men and women who will pray in faith, believing He is faithful and true to His word. Men and women who will go to the door, receive His promise and pray through to completion the fulfillment, the manifestation, of His promise. Will you pray?

Let us hold fast the confession of our hope without wavering, for He who promised is faithful.

HEBREWS 10:23 (NKJV)

Let us Pray!

ARTICLE 6

WHAT DO YOU THINK?

What do you think? This is a simple enough question, one you might hear several times in a day. It is also a question you should ask yourself. So, in general what do you think? Maybe it would be better to say, how do you think? When you meet someone for the first time, when the phone rings at night, when your boss comes to your office, what do you think? Do you think the worst, or do you think the best?

It is easy to think the worst; this is how the world thinks and tries to train us to think. Everyone talks about the worst. We have hundreds of expression in the English language to express the worst. Often people don't even know they are saying something that expresses the worst, it is just an expression. But expressions, talk, ads, movies, songs, and hundreds of other parts of modern western living, focus on thinking the worst. The world may think the worst, but as Christians we are to think the best.

I hope you always believe the best about me. As the editor of *Voice of Thanksgiving*, the newsletter of this company of believers, I strive to hear from God as I call you to prayer. I hope that you will hear my heart, even if I make a mistake in my writing—and some of you are good at pointing out my mistakes—knowing that my intention is good. This is not a request for sympathy; I use myself to make a point. Knowing that David loves the Lord, knowing that he longs to have a company of people who pray and are effective in prayer, and knowing that his intention is for the best, I hope you will believe the best. Sure, point out errors and mistakes, I also want to be a better communicator, but do not be offended if I make a mistake. Think the best, not the worst. Think David has made a mistake, but think the best. Now I hope I have made my point, think the best.

With that said, now we can turn to the central theme of this message; think the best, but pray the Word. As much as I have encouraged you to think the best, when you pray, don't just think the best, instead pray the word. Let's continue to use me for an example. When you pray for me, and I hope you do pray for me although I should be a long way down on your priority list of prayers, your family, your church, your pastor, and many other things should be higher on the list than me. But, when you pray for me, don't pray based on thinking the best about me. You should think the best about me when you read the *Voice of Thanksgiving*; but when you pray, pray the Word. Don't pray, "I know David is a good guy". Think the best, but don't pray like I am the best. When you pray, pray what God says. Pray things like, "David has the mind of Christ", why because the Word say it is true, not because David is good.

> *For "who has known the mind of the Lord that he may instruct Him?" But we have the mind of Christ.*
>
> I CORINTHIANS 2:16 (NKJV)

Let this mind be in you which was also in Christ Jesus,

PHILIPPIANS 2:5 (NKJV)

This is not a study on how to pray for me, it is a call for a self-check on your prayers. When you pray do you agree with man and believe the worst or believe the best and pray as though the person is the best? Either of these can be wrong. When we pray, what is important is what the Word of God says. The format for your prayers is your own choosing, but the key to success is agreement with God. Prayer in agreement with God, agreement with His Word, is world changing.

Daniel was a mighty man of prayer because he prayed what God said. It was time for Israel to return to their homeland, the required seventy years accomplished. So Daniel prayed. What did he pray? Did he pray, "The Jews are your favorite people and they are so good, they are the best, so take them back to their home land". No. He knew they had sinned and turned from God. He still prayed for them, he continued to think the best. However, he prayed not based on Israel's goodness, but on what God had declared for Israel. He prayed the Word.

> *Then I set my face toward the Lord God to make request by prayer and supplications, with fasting, sackcloth, and ashes. And I prayed to the Lord my God, and made confession, and said, "O Lord, great and awesome God, who keeps His covenant and mercy with those who love Him, and with those who keep His commandments, we have sinned and committed iniquity, we have done wickedly and rebelled, even by departing from Your precepts and Your judgments.*

> DANIEL 9:3-5 (NKJV)

"O Lord, according to all Your righteousness, I pray, let Your anger and Your fury be turned away from Your city Jerusalem, Your holy mountain; because for our sins, and for the iniquities of our fathers, Jerusalem and Your people are a reproach to all those around us. Now therefore, our God, hear the prayer of Your servant, and his supplications, and for the Lord's sake cause Your face to shine on Your sanctuary, which is desolate. O my God, incline Your ear and hear; open Your eyes and see our desolations, and the city which is called by Your name; for we do not present our supplications before You because of our righteous deeds, but because of Your great mercies. O Lord, hear! O Lord, forgive! O Lord, listen and act! Do not delay for Your own sake, my God, for Your city and Your people are called by Your name."

DANIEL 9:16-19 (NKJV)

We live in a time like that of Daniel, a time of great struggle. People often think and do the worst. The need for God and His salvation is as important as it was in Daniel's time. If we are going to see the people delivered from captivity, we must pray like Daniel. We must think the best, but not pray based on thinking they are the best. We must pray with prayers based on what God's Word says.

Let us Pray!

ARTICLE 7

BELIEVE

I n reading my books or the articles of the newsletter *Voice of Thanksgiving*, you may have noticed I like the stories of the Bible. When I was a little boy I was blessed to attend good Sunday School classes. The teachers (including times when the teachers were my mom and dad) made the stories of the Bible come alive. Week after week there was a story from the Bible. With these stories they taught us the great truths of the Christian faith. They also taught us the value of the Bible as a guide for proper living and success. I loved the stories and tried to apply the lessons.

One of the most widely known of the Bible stories is the Last Supper. In this story, we see Jesus' continued teaching of the nature of a servant and the institution of Communion. Before the main story begins there is an unusual part of the story. When asked where they should prepare for the Passover supper, Jesus tells them to look for a man carrying a jar of water. The disciples went into the city and found the man just as Jesus had described and they were taken to a prepared room.

This part of the story is much more than just window dressing for the supper; it has a powerful lesson, for us, of its own.

The most important word in the Christian life is faith. We are Born Again by faith, we must live by faith, and effective prayer is by faith. It is impossible to please God without faith. Faith is the keystone to life and gaining knowledge of and understanding of faith is a lifetime learning process. Just as my Sunday School teachers had another lesson for us to learn every week, year-after-year, so the Holy Spirit has many new lessons on faith for us to learn. One of these lessons is found in the beginning of the story about the Last Supper.

> *Then came the Day of Unleavened Bread, when the Passover must be killed. And He sent Peter and John, saying, "Go and prepare the Passover for us, that we may eat." So they said to Him, "Where do You want us to prepare?" And He said to them, "Behold, when you have entered the city, a man will meet you carrying a pitcher of water; follow him into the house which he enters. Then you shall say to the master of the house, 'The Teacher says to you, "Where is the guest room where I may eat the Passover with My disciples?"' Then he will show you a large, furnished upper room; there make ready." So they went and found it just as He had said to them, and they prepared the Passover.*
>
> LUKE 22:7-13 (NKJV)

This lesson on faith is centered on the concept of believing. Jesus said there would be a man in the town. Jesus said he would direct them to a place for the supper. It would have been easy to dismiss Jesus in this case. A man carrying a jar and a house prepared for them, this is unusual. The disciples believed Jesus at His word and went into town and found things just as Jesus had described them. Believing is the beginning of faith.

Faith believes God. Faith believes Him at His Word. Faith believes His word is His bond. Faith believes that what God has said, He will do. Faith is the key to success, and progress in the Christian life is by faith. This is true for the prayer life as well. When we come to Him in prayer we must come by faith, we must believe God.

> *But without faith it is impossible to please Him, for he*
> *who comes to God must believe that He is, and that He is*
> *a rewarder of those who diligently seek Him.*
> HEBREWS 11:6 (NKJV)

Faith is necessary and this verse addresses two requirements. First, we must believe that God is God. That means we must believe God is the all powerful being that He claims to be. Second, we must believe that God rewards those diligently seeking Him. The key here is, we must believe.

The first requirement seems easy enough; all that is necessary is for people to believe that God is God. However, we find that this can be a stumbling block. In the American capitol city, there is a massive building at the end of the main mall. Across the front of this building are huge columns and behind these columns, high above the mall, is a statue of President Abraham Lincoln. Lincoln was the 16th president of the United States and he led America through its Civil War. Lincoln is listed by many people as one of the best, if not the best president of American history. The statue is bigger than life and makes Lincoln into almost a god like figure. To see him can be inspiring, but he does not do anything; he just sits there.

Many people believe in a God who is like this statue of Lincoln. He is most assuredly God, but He just sits in Heaven.

However, this view does not meet the reality of the nature of God as presented in the Bible. In Hebrews 11:6 we are told to believe God is. We must believe that He is who He says he is and He can do what He says He can do. Believing anything less than this does not met the requirement for being a believer. God is involved in the life of His people and He answers prayers; this is the God revealed in the Bible. If we try to limit Him to less than this, if we try to limit God's ability to act with us and for us, we have stopped believing that He is God.

> *Do you have faith? Have it to yourself before God. Happy*
> *is he who does not condemn himself in what he approves.*
> ROMANS 14:22 (NKJV)

The second requirement requires us to believe as well. In this part we must believe that God is a rewarder of those who seek Him. Hebrews 11:6 makes it clear that if we diligently seek Him, God will reward us. The Hebrew words used for the phrase "diligently seek" means to search out, investigate, crave, demand, or worship.

There is a lot to diligently seeking God in prayer. True prayer is searching out God's will, His nature, and promises. Prayer is working for God's kingdom to come here on earth as it is in Heaven. Prayer is seeking the application and fulfillment of His word in our life and in those around us. Prayer is worshiping God for who and what He is. Prayer is also requesting and receiving answers to meet our needs and those of others.

To have faith we must believe and we must believe correctly. We need to examine ourselves and check what we believe. Do we limit God? Do we fail to ask or ask amiss because we view God through glasses that see Him limited? Do we seek Him with our whole heart, soul, mind, and strength?

If we are to be successful in prayer we must believe. We must believe that God is God and able and willing to do what He has said and we must believe that He rewards those who pray. Every day we face opportunities like the disciples looking for the place for the supper. As these opportunities come we can limit God or we can believe and by faith receive God's provision. It pleases God if we have faith and believe.

Let us Pray!

GOD IS ABLE TO PERFORM

Evidence is an important part of our life. We demand it in many arenas like court cases and scientific exploration. It is based on the evidence that a jury should make a decision or a scientist a conclusion in an experiment. And we should use evidence in making important decisions. Often you hear people say something like, "Look at the evidence", if the evidence shows there will be a positive result, it is a good plan. If the evidence shows there will be a negative result, it is a bad plan.

We tend to tell people they acted foolishly when they did not pay attention to the evidence. We do this a lot with young people. For example, the evidence is very strong that drinking and driving is dangerous; a young person, or anyone else, who drinks and then drives is acting foolishly. Looking at the evidence is a valued part of society, but it can destroy faith.

Abraham, a great man of faith, had come to a point where there was strong evidence that he would not have any children. Not only had he and his wife not had children, but their time for bearing children had passed. The evidence showed that they would never have children. This is the type of evidence that often destroys a man's faith. However, even with all this evidence against him, Abraham believed God. God had made a promise to Abraham and this man of faith did not let the body of evidence cause a faltering of his faith.

In the book of Romans, in the Bible, we read that, Abraham did not waver at the promise of God through unbelief. Abraham looked at the evidence and weighed it against the promise of God and he was fully convinced that God would do what He promised. He believed God's promises were able to overcome the expected outcome based on the evidence. Abraham had faith in God.

> *And not being weak in faith, he did not consider his own body, already dead (since he was about a hundred years old), and the deadness of Sarah's womb. He did not waver at the promise of God through unbelief, but was strengthened in faith, giving glory to God, and being fully convinced that what He had promised He was also able to perform.*
>
> ROMANS 4:19-21 (NKJV)

In the previous article we began to explore faith, looking at the faith required for effective prayer. The faith for obtaining answers to prayers. Our focus was on the verse from Hebrews that demands two things for coming to God; believing that God is and believing that God rewards those who seek Him.

> *But without faith it is impossible to please Him, for he who comes to God must believe that He is, and that He is a rewarder of those who diligently seek Him.*
>
> HEBREWS 11:6 (NKJV)

In that article we explored the meaning of the phrase, believing that God is. It is easy to believe that God is God as long as God is just a general term. It is more difficult when we face believing that this means that God can do what He claims He can do, in our life and in our prayers. His claims throughout the Bible are amazing and quite radical. He claims to be able to do all we ask or imagine and then more. He claims to be able to do things that physical evidence claims cannot be done. When God can go beyond the restrictions of evidence, people have trouble believing that God is God. And this weakens and can destroy their faith.

> *Jesus said to him, "If you can believe, all things are possible to him who believes."*
>
> MARK 9:23 (NKJV)

> *Let us hold fast the profession of our faith without wavering; (for he is faithful that promised;)*
>
> HEBREWS 10:23 (KJV)

The Bible declares, in no uncertain terms, that God is able to work beyond the rules of natural law and the dictates of evidence. The man of faith must believe God over the evidence. Abraham knew the evidence. This was not theoretical to him, he lived it day-by-day. He lived in the body of evidence! He was an old man and he knew that Sarah's womb was as good as dead. That was the evidence; it would stand up in any court of law. The difference between Abraham, the man of faith, and most people today, is that Abraham looked to God. Abraham saw God's promises and abilities as overriding the evidence at hand.

Many years ago there was a cartoon that showed two scientists standing in front of a huge blackboard. The board was covered with scientific notation. You could tell that the scientists were following through the notation that described some great event or experiment. In the caption one scientist explains to the other, "This happens, then this happens, and then something miraculous happens here."

This is a description of faith. There is evidence for this and this, but there comes a time when we cannot explain what happened. When the unexplainable happens, it is often God moving miraculously. The problem is too often we do not allow the miraculous to happen. We destroy faith rather than allowing God to move miraculously. We simply do not believe that God is God and able to do what He has said.

I have said for years that we must look at the evidence, this is important, only a fool would not look at the evidence. However, we must not let the evidence dictate the end result. We must look at the evidence and treat it like the numbers in an equation. Put all the numbers in a calculator, that is punch in all the evidence, and then push the special button, the God button. By that I mean, the final result is not just what the evidence says, we must let God move beyond the evidence and gain His desired result.

He changes the times and season. He moves mountains. He melts and molds the hearts of men. He stops the march of mighty armies. He rises up and casts down nations. Why do we have trouble believing He can move miraculously on behalf of our prayers?

Faith comes by hearing the Word of God. Faith that believes God can and will do what He has said He will do. If we are going to pray effective fervent prayers, prayers that avail much, we must build on faith. We must hear what God has been saying. It is as though He says "I am God and I can and will move for those who will by faith believe that I am God. I can and will do what I said I will do". We must walk in expectation of seeing God move powerfully in answer to prayer.

Father, we are not going to be weak in faith, we will not let evidence dictate to us the answers to our prayers. We will not waver at Your promises. We will not let unbelief rule our prayers. God we give You all the glory and are fully convinced that what You have promised, You are able to perform.

Let us Pray!

BUILDING A DEPTH OF FAITH

I n the National Park near our home there is a place I love to go. The place is beautiful and restful. Through the middle of this lovely scene runs a small stream. The stream meanders along between willow bushes and in some of its curves the water is very deep. The deep water is beautiful and important for the river. The area where this stream flows gets very dry and by mid summer, most years, this stream is down to just a few inches of water. To survive, fish must live in the curves of the river in the deep pockets of water. Success in prayer also requires deep pockets, deep pockets of faith.

Christians who pray know that to pray effectively we need faith. The world with its life numbing rituals, brain draining demands, and convoluted thinking, destroys faith. For success in prayer we must have faith and faith comes from the Word of God. Christians know God's promises stand firm and true; He has promised that we can have faith!

This has always been God's way, His way of faith. He is building faith in all who will receive from Him. Faith comes by hearing His Word and if we are going to be effective in prayer, then the lessons of faith, must make their mark on our life and our prayers. Prayer without faith is just a religious exercise, but prayer with faith moves mountains.

Our walk of faith must be like the stream I described with the deep pockets of water. Day-by-day we need to move closer to God, deeper in His embrace, deeper in His love, deeper in His care, and deeper in his power and might. In addition, and of great importance, we must go deeper and deeper in faith. If we are to pray and accomplish all God has called us to do, we must live in pockets of deep faith. We must live, walk, and be strong in faith, deep faith.

Let us pray!

> *He did not waver at the promise of God through unbelief, but was strengthened in faith, giving glory to God, and being fully convinced that what He had promised He was also able to perform.*
>
> ROMANS 4:20-21 (NKJV)

In these verses we read that Abraham was strengthened in faith. The word translated here as "strengthened" means to increase in strength. We need to have an increase in strength in the area of faith, building deep faith so we can pray effective, fervent prayers that avail much. The articles in this unit explore the strengthening and deepening of our faith.

ARTICLE 9

STYLE AND SUBSTANCE

Recorded in the Bible we find sketches of the life of famous and infamous kings. The life of these kings makes for very interesting stories and valuable character and faith studies. Two of the kings, Saul and David, are perhaps the most famous. These two kings were poles apart and are a good representation of the differences between style and substance. Saul was style and David substance.

Saul was all style; taller than others, he did everything in grand style. He was a king that gave the people a show. When Samuel warned the people about what having a king would entail; the list is all about style. Samuel tells them that the king will take men, women, and fruits of their fields and work, all to provide and maintain the splendor and style of King Saul (see 1 Samuel 8:10-17).

Saul came to every event with the flash and fuss, the important thing was looking good and maintaining his style. However, it was style that got him into trouble. When Samuel was late coming to the sacrifice, Saul decided to do it himself. Why was Saul in a hurry? He was king, what caused him to feel a need to rush things and thus to get into trouble? The answer is style; Samuel being late was cramping King Saul's style. He did not want to look bad in front of the people. Style was more important to Saul than substance.

In contrast, King David, who had his faults, was focused on substance. He did not have credentials of looking like a king or making a show of everything. Notice that when God describes David, He honors him by calling him a man after His own heart. God also states that David did God's will.

> *And when He had removed him, He raised up for them*
> *David as king, to whom also He gave testimony and said,*
> *'I have found David the son of Jesse, a man after My own*
> *heart, who will do all My will.'*
>
> ACTS 13:22 (NKJV)

If we want to be a man after God's heart, we must do God's will. This is still God's requirement and the standard that must be met today. David's life was doing the will of God. Even when King David made mistakes he was quick to repent, make amends, and do things correctly. For example, he decided to move the Ark of God. The first time David did things his own way and it turned out very bad. One of David's friends was killed. However, David repented of his sin and then did things God's way and there was a great blessing for David and the people. Even the so called show of style, as they brought the Ark through the streets, was not show. It was simply David praising God with all his might.

> *Then David danced before the Lord with all his might;*
> *and David was wearing a linen ephod. So David and all*
> *the house of Israel brought up the ark of the Lord with*
> *shouting and with the sound of the trumpet.*
>
> 2 SAMUEL 6:14-15 (NKJV)

Style is just the basic appearance of things. It lacks the reality and power of whatever it portrays. It can be beautiful, but upon examination there is nothing of the fundamental nature there; it is just the form of the matter. Substance is the reality; it is the essential nature. In life there is a battle raging between style and substance. This is a struggle that everyone faces in one way or another.

The world we live in is strong on style and weak on substance. Too often people have gone for style over substance; just as ancient Israel did when they followed King Saul. This leads to many problems, including problems in our Christian life and our prayer life. If all we have, or even if most of what we have, is just style, then we have no power for living, working, or in prayer. The insidious nature of style is that its illusion can be so strong we think we have something, when we do not. For example, if I have only a style of faith and not the substance, I do not have faith.

E. M. Bounds in some of his writings had a list of what he deemed to be the essentials of successful prayer. It would be good for us to look at these essentials and make use of what we could call a Style and Substance Test. The test is an examination of our life, by rating our level of style compared to substance. For each of these essentials, do we have style or do we have substance, the real thing, active and working in our life?

In my classroom when I gave a test, students would receive a "0" for the test if a friend whispered answers to them (or passed notes, or showed them their answers, etc.). However, on this test it is okay, actually it is best, if the Holy Spirit whispers answers to you. His assessment is more accurate than anything we can do without His help.

I encourage you to take the test, it is simple to do, and let the Holy Spirit help you assess your level of style or substance.

The test is simple; there is a range of answers, pick where you fall in the range. On the one side of the range is style and moving along toward the other side is more and more substance, until you reach fully substance. The choices are: all style, a little style, half style and half substance, mostly substance, or all substance. This is not an exact test, but can be valuable. Please remember there is no condemnation; we are learning and tests are part of the learning process.

Are you ready for the test? For each of the following essentials from E. M. Bounds' list, place yourself within a range. For each are you more style or substance? Here is the list: Faith, trust, desire, fervency, persistence, good character and conduct, obedience, and vigilance. Ready, set, go!

How did you do? Are there areas where you are more style than substance? Are there areas where you need to make changes and improvements? If we long to make real changes in our life, we can; the Holy Spirit will work with us and we can go to the Holy Spirit School of Prayer until we are established in the substance of each and every aspect of prayer. It can be hard work, but it yields great results. We can move from style to substance and as we do, we will pray more effective, fervent prayers that avail much.

Let us Pray!

DEPTH

As a boy growing up I enjoyed fishing. My family enjoyed fishing, so it was easy to get everyone excited about going several times every summer. My father and Grandfathers were great fishermen and they taught me well. We enjoyed trout fishing on little streams in the mountains of Colorado so we never branched out into other types of fishing. Dropping a fly on a beaver pond and seeing a trout leap out of the water after that fly is a thrill that is hard to beat. The beauty of the Colorado Rockies, the joy of catching trout, and the great family times, made fishing a special part of my life.

There were many places I loved to fish; beaver ponds on the western slope, streams meandering through a mountain valley, and small rivers along the eastern slope of the Front Range. These are the places I went as a boy. One spot was very special. My Grandparents had a cabin in the mountains and I would go and stay with them several times during the summer. My Grandfather and I would go out early in the evening and get a fish or two for my Grandmother for breakfast.

Near their cabin there was a spot that was a little different from most of the streams we fished. This spot twisted around a large rock, this caused a very deep pool of water. This was a spot that could support large fish. Most of the fish we caught on this stream were 6 to 12 inches long, but there are places on the stream where there were larger fish and this was one of those places.

One day my brother Bill and I worked this spot. We caught a few small fish, but we just could not get that big one. Finally, after fishing for a long time, Bill hooked a big fish. Very quickly we knew this was a much larger fish than we were accustomed to and it would be a great challenge to land this fish. He worked and worked, keeping constant pressure on the line so the hook would not slip out, but not pulling too hard and breaking the line. Little by little he brought this fish in. It was huge compared to the fish we normally caught on this stream. It was very exciting to see how he did it and then to see this great fish.

Jesus has always had a special fondness for fishermen. A number of His first disciples were fishermen. Throughout history He has been calling for and then blessing men and women who would be like those first disciples and become fishers of men. Even today He is calling for fishermen. In a very real way His call is to all Christians, He calls all of us to fish with Him. Specifically, this call is to work the harvest fields, bring men and women to the Father, for receiving salvation in Christ Jesus. No man comes to the Father except the Holy Sprit draws them. However, He, the Holy Spirit, uses men and women, like us, to work the fields with Him and a key to success in this work is prayer.

Bringing people to Christ begins with prayer. The great evangelistic movements of the last 20 centuries have had there origins in prayer. The great ministries of this period have been birthed and nurtured by prayer. Just as a fisherman uses rod and reel to catch fish, so the Holy Spirit uses prayer. And His use of prayer depends on men or women of prayer. There are two key factors that determine how He can work with a person of prayer. The first is the depth of faith and the second is the depth of commitment.

In that mountain stream where I liked to fish, most of the stream would not support large fish. There was not enough depth of water to provide the habitat needed for a large fish. The stream was good for fish, it met the needs of a trout very well, but most of this stream did not have the depth that was needed for a large fish. That is why the spot I described earlier was so special. It was one of the few places where this stream could support larger fish.

Prayer is like that stream. Most people who pray have little depth of faith. This lack of depth limits their usefulness in prayer. Prayer is an exercise and expression of faith. Too many people try to pray without faith in God or His willingness and ability to answer prayer. And without faith it is impossible to please God.

> But without faith it is impossible to please Him, for he who comes to God must believe that He is, and that He is a rewarder of those who diligently seek Him.
>
> HEBREWS 11:6 (NKJV)

Success in prayer comes by faith. Prayer without faith is just words. It is like a swirl of snow on a cold, cloudy day. The snow flits along here and there, moved by every breath of wind. By contrast, prayer with faith is solid and powerful, it can move mountains.

So Jesus answered and said to them, "Assuredly, I say to you, if you have faith and do not doubt, you will not only do what was done to the fig tree, but also if you say to this mountain, 'Be removed and be cast into the sea,' it will be done."

MATTHEW 21:21 (NKJV)

People who are mature in prayer, men and women who have been nurtured by the lessons of the Holy Sprit, have a depth of faith. This deep faith opens doors of opportunity and the Holy Spirit can call on these people for increasingly tougher assignments in prayer.

When Bill hooked that big fish, there were many ways he could loose him. I am not the fisherman my brother is, so it is quite likely that I would have reacted poorly to this challenge. I would have jerked the line so hard I would have broken it and ended the one chance we had to catch this fish. Bill, on the other hand, knew what to do. His depth of knowledge and skill in fishing helped him work this fish slowly, but consistently, out of the depths of the water and the pull of the current of the stream; drawing the fish to the shore.

Bill had great depth of skill in fishing and was the right man for the job. God is looking for the right man or woman for the job of prayer. The Holy Spirit is looking for men and women who have learned about faith and developed their faith. He is looking for people who will and can pray about difficult situations and exercise their deep faith to receive an answer.

There was another key factor in our success in landing that big fish that day. Bill had a depth of commitment. Most of the fish we caught were caught with a quick flip of the wrist. From the moment we presented the bait, to the moment we land the fish, was just a few seconds. However, the day we caught the big fish, it took a great deal of time. Not only did Bill have to continue on for a long time, but he had to continue the skilled actions throughout this relatively long period.

At times people will get excited about prayer. They begin to pray, but if the answer does not come quickly their commitment wanes and they stop. Once again the Holy Spirit is left holding the bag. He was looking for a prayer warrior and got a prayer wimp. Some people teach that all we need is faith. If we ask believing, then this prayer is a done deal. There is a great deal of truth in their teachings, but the Bible also teaches about a depth of commitment. There are assignments that the Holy Spirit gives that demand a depth of both faith and commitment.

> *I have set watchmen on your walls, O Jerusalem; They shall never hold their peace day or night. You who make mention of the Lord, do not keep silent,*
>
> ISAIAH 62:6 (NKJV)

> *I say to you, though he will not rise and give to him because he is his friend, yet because of his persistence he will rise and give him as many as he needs.*
>
> LUKE 11:8 (NKJV)

> *Then He spoke a parable to them, that men always ought to pray and not lose heart,*
>
> LUKE 18:1 (NKJV)

Depth of faith and depth of commitment, the man or woman, who is useful for the Holy Spirit, will have both. The Holy Spirit is looking for candidates for His lessons in effective prayer. Not excluding anyone, because everyone can pray, but the Holy Spirit is seeking men and women of prayer, ready and able to be given any assignment. These assignments come to a man or woman with deep faith, faith so deep he or she can believe for anything. These assignments come to the man or woman who the Holy Spirit knows will make and keep their commitment. The Holy Spirit assigns important prayers to those who will continue to pray no matter what comes and continue with faith.

Where do you stand in faith and commitment? What can the Holy Spirit put on your plate? Is there sufficient depth to meet the challenges of faith and commitment? What need, what condition, what situation, can He entrust to you and your prayers?

Let us Pray!

FORGIVENESS

When I was a teenager, I bought some books from a company by mail. It was a program where they sent out books; if I liked them, I kept them and paid for them. The first books were fine, but then there were some problems. I tried to stop the program and they did not want to stop. The situation ended badly and this left a bad taste in my mouth. For years I vowed that I would never buy books or anything else from this company.

A few months ago I was watching TV and noticed a commercial for some music CDs produced by this company. This was the company I had dealt with many years ago. I changed the channel and then realized that I was still angry with this company. For more than 35 years I had been angry with this company. That was not good; I had to deal with the anger and I also had to forgive. This was very hard for me.

Let all bitterness, wrath, anger, clamor, and evil speaking be put away from you, with all malice. And be kind to

one another, tenderhearted, forgiving one another, just as
God in Christ forgave you.

EPHESIANS 4:31-32 (NKJV)

Looking back at this, it was not that big of a deal, but once I was hurt, or felt I was hurt, I was against them. What I needed to do was forgive. There needed to be forgiveness on my part, to help them, and to help me. Dealing with unforgiveness is important. Unforgiveness keeps us from God and limits our power in prayer.

For if you forgive men their trespasses, your heavenly
Father will also forgive you. But if you do not forgive men
their trespasses, neither will your Father forgive your
trespasses.

MATTHEW 6:14-15 (NKJV)

Without faith our prayers will fail; unforgiveness, unbelief, doubt, anger, and other sins hinder or even destroy our faith. One of the most important of these sins is unforgiveness. Unforgiveness is like a wall of separation between us and our Father. Unforgiveness also opens the door to other sins such as anger and doubt and one of the keys for success in prayer is to keep from doubting.

Beware, brethren, lest there be in any of you an evil heart
of unbelief in departing from the living God; but exhort
one another daily, while it is called "Today," lest any of
you be hardened through the deceitfulness of sin.

HEBREWS 3:12-13 (NKJV)

But let him ask in faith, with no doubting, for he who
doubts is like a wave of the sea driven and tossed by the
wind.

JAMES 1:6 (NKJV)

> So Jesus answered and said to them, "Have faith in God.
> For assuredly, I say to you, whoever says to this mountain,
> 'Be removed and be cast into the sea,' and does not doubt
> in his heart, but believes that those things he says will be
> done, he will have whatever he says. Therefore I say to
> you, whatever things you ask when you pray, believe that
> you receive them, and you will have them. "And whenever
> you stand praying, if you have anything against anyone,
> forgive him, that your Father in heaven may also forgive
> you your trespasses. But if you do not forgive, neither will
> your Father in heaven forgive your trespasses."

MARK 11:22-26 (NKJV)

Forgiveness is a key to successful, effective prayer; this can be a struggle for many people. Unforgiveness is a roadblock to faith; it often hinders a fruitful life and receiving answers to prayer. Too often we only give lip service to forgiveness. We say, "I forgive you," but in our heart we have judged, brought a guilty plea, and are ready to bring a sentence. On the inside we are saying, "God get him". This is not forgiveness and it limits our prayers.

True forgiveness, by contrast, is coming to the point where even in our heart, we desire God's blessing for the person who has wronged us. When we can pray with honesty and fervency for a blessing for the other person, just as we would pray for a blessing for our self, then we have forgiven.

> So My heavenly Father also will do to you if each of
> you, from his heart, does not forgive his brother his
> trespasses."

MATTHEW 18:35 (NKJV)

It is important for us to search our hearts, by the guidance of the Holy Spirit, to see if we are holding unforgiveness against someone or some group. Forgiveness requires a change of heart (ask the Father for help with this) and it may take action on your part (ask the Holy Spirit for direction of proper actions). For effective praying, forgive. Break the chains that have held you captive; seek a blessing for the other person. With the chains off, you are free to seek God with all of your heart, in fullness of faith.

Let us Pray!

DO NOT DOUBT

For many years I coached football (American football). It is interesting to look back on the teams that I coached. Each year as coaches, we would look at the talent of the team and estimate how we thought the team would do. Some of the teams I coached had a realistic chance of doing well, other years a realistic appraisal suggested that we would struggle to win very many games.

Sports teams are interesting to compare. There are teams who know in their heart that they will struggle throughout the year; they may win some games, but the season will be a struggle. Other teams believe they will do well and win their games, but when things get difficult there is a nagging doubt about winning. There are other teams who know they will win. There was a local team that won three state titles in a row. They knew they would win. Even in games where they fell way behind, this team would find a way to win and week after week they did (sometimes right at the end of the game). They never doubted that they would win.

One of the most predominant faith destroyers is doubt. The application of faith is a key component to success in prayer. We know that with faith we can expect to see our prayers avail much. The problem is that there are things that can hinder or even destroy our faith and thus make us ineffective in prayer.

> *So Jesus answered and said to them, "Have faith in God.*
> *For assuredly, I say to you, whoever says to this mountain,*
> *'Be removed and be cast into the sea,' and does not doubt*
> *in his heart, but believes that those things he says will be*
> *done, he will have whatever he says. Therefore I say to you,*
> *whatever things you ask when you pray, believe that you*
> *receive them, and you will have them.*
>
> MARK 11:22-24 (NKJV)

Like those football teams I described, what is in our heart makes a big difference. Sure a football team with no talent would have a hard time beating a team that had great talent, but it is the attitude of the heart that often makes the difference between winning and losing. In prayer dealing with doubt in our heart makes the difference between effective prayers that avail much and prayers that fall to the ground; spoken, but unanswered.

Jesus repeatedly dealt with the problem of doubt. He said that if we do not doubt in our heart, we could have whatever we ask. The problem is that most people are like the teams that think they can win, but there is a nagging doubt that hides in their heart until an opportune moment. People pray and believe that they will receive the answer, but doubt does its work and faith fades.

> *So He said, "Come." And when Peter had come down out*
> *of the boat, he walked on the water to go to Jesus. But*
> *when he saw that the wind was boisterous, he was afraid;*

and beginning to sink he cried out, saying, "Lord, save me!" And immediately Jesus stretched out His hand and caught him, and said to him, "O you of little faith, why did you doubt?"

MATTHEW 14:29-31 (NKJV)

We pray and expect to have an answer (I hope you expect answers when you pray!). If the answers come quickly, great, but if not, hindrances may come to beset our faith. If the answer does not come immediately we may begin to worry, question, and doubt. Like little foxes nipping at us, things come to fight against our faith. If we are not careful, doubt will swallow up our faith. However, this does not have to be the result; we can and should fight back.

But you, O man of God, flee these things and pursue righteousness, godliness, faith, love, patience, gentleness. Fight the good fight of faith, lay hold on eternal life, to which you were also called and have confessed the good confession in the presence of many witnesses.

I TIMOTHY 6:11-12 (NKJV)

At some point in this battle our hearts will be tested. If doubt is found in our heart it can limit or even destroy our faith and there will be few, if any answers to our prayers. On the other hand, if no doubt is found in our heart and if we stand firm to the end, we have God's promise that answers will come!

The key is our heart. Guarding our heart is crucial. It is a key to success. Out of our heart come the issues of life and the most important issue is faith. Take a look at an example of the importance of the heart and its protection.

Keep your heart with all diligence, For out of it spring the issues of life.

PROVERBS 4:23 (NKJV)

Please note that in the verses surrounding this verse from Proverbs, there are several keys to protecting the heart. This is a list of steps to take to keep out doubt. How many specific instructions can you see in these words of advice from a father to his son? Or more specifically, how many instructions can you find in this advice from our Heavenly Father to us?

My son, give attention to my words; Incline your ear to my sayings. Do not let them depart from your eyes; Keep them in the midst of your heart; For they are life to those who find them, And health to all their flesh. Keep your heart with all diligence, For out of it spring the issues of life. Put away from you a deceitful mouth, And put perverse lips far from you. Let your eyes look straight ahead, And your eyelids look right before you. Ponder the path of your feet, And let all your ways be established. Do not turn to the right or the left; Remove your foot from evil.

PROVERBS 4:20-27 (NKJV)

How many instructions did you find? Here are a few that I noted. First, He tells us to pay attention to the Bible. To pay attention to it, we must read it, study it, memorize it, speak it, and meditate on what God has said. Casual reading and occasional study is not enough to keep out doubt.

Second, we need to listen to what God is saying. Too often people read the Bible and like the man looking in the mirror, who then forgets what he looks like, they read and forget. We are to listen carefully and with the intention of doing what God says to do. And then do what He says.

Third, to keep out doubt, we must regularly review what He has said. Every day is not too soon for review. Better yet is a moment-by-moment review. Unfortunately living in the world drains us of the word and faith; yesterday's infilling of the Word of God is not enough for today. Every day we need a refill.

Fourth, with a daily infilling of the Word, we must hold on to the Word of God, treasuring it in our heart. In the human body the heart pumps blood to the entire body and the blood carries nourishment to the body, however, it only pumps what it has. In the spiritual world, the heart works the same way; it pumps nourishment to the entire body. If we do not fill our heart with God's Word, we are allowing other things to enter into our heart. It will faithfully pump to our body the supply of what it has to pump. Fill it with His Word, and it will pump the Word, the antidote for doubt.

This is a great list, but there is more. The fifth instruction is very simple to say, watch your mouth! It is harder to do. Do not say things that are not what God says. Regardless of the situation or the difficulties you face, say what God says.

Sixth, the world presents allurements, there are many designed with you in mind. Do not be lured away by looking at the world. Guard against situations that would destroy your faith or separate you from God. Regardless of what happens the true reality is what God says. Stay true to Him, say what He says.

Seventh, there is a path for the Christian to follow, a path that follows the guidance of the Lord. This is a special place in His presence and power, specially made for us. Stay on this path and do not chase after evil in any form. To stay on this path we need to meditate on and practice walking in what God says.

*A good man out of the good treasure of his heart brings
forth good; and an evil man out of the evil treasure of his
heart brings forth evil. For out of the abundance of the
heart his mouth speaks.*

LUKE 6:45 (NKJV)

Prayer is so simple, have faith in God, keep doubt out of
your heart, and you will receive the answer. Unfortunately, it
takes effort to have faith and it takes effort to keep doubt out
of our heart. For those who will make the effort and do things
God's way, there is a wonderful world of prayer they can tap
into. Will you make the effort and do what He says, in guarding your heart and in action? If so, you can pray effective, faith
filled prayers that avail much. You can say to the mountain, be
removed, and it will be cast into the sea.

Let us Pray!

DOORS AND WINDOWS

It seems as though every week I am telling you about something that happened in my past. And it is true. I had a good childhood; my parents loved me and cared for me and even the "bad" incidents were not all that bad. Having Christian parents is a great blessing. So it is easy and pleasant for me to remember simpler, easier times. For example, there were many summers when I was a boy we would leave the front door open to let the cool air come in. All we had to do at night was just hook the screen door.

Let me explain. In the place where I grew up the weather changes a great deal from summer to winter. Days in the summer can be very hot and in the winter it can be very cold. In the summer we would open the doors and windows to let what breeze there was, come in and cool the house. In the winter time we would close everything and even cover cracks around the frame of the doors and windows to try to keep the cold out. With that background information we can get back to the screen door in the summer time.

Where I grew up, we felt safe enough to just hook the screen door, so it would not blow open if there was some wind. We did not have to worry about break-ins and other threats. We did not have to have steel doors, multiple locks, and alarm systems.

Dealing with the heat was the problem in the summer, but it was the cold drafts in the winter. On cold nights, there was a draft through the edge of some of the windows and doors. When it got very cold we would shove a blanket up against the base of the door to keep more of the cold air out. We did not have double pane windows with special gas in between the panes to increase the "R" value of the windows.

Doors and windows are important to a house, they provide a point of contact with the outside world (and with the outside weather) and they can be very useful. The value of the door or window depends on how they serve us when we use them. If the door or window serves us well, it is of good value, if it does not serve us well, it is of poor value.

In a similar way the doors and windows of our heart are the point of contact with the spiritual world. We have control over how the contact is used. The point of contact of our heart can serve us well, for example, we can use it to make contact with the spiritual world of the Father, Son, and the Holy Spirit. Alternately, this point of contact of our heart, these same doors and windows, can be used for contact with the world of evil, death, and destruction.

Giving access to the blessings of the Father is the way we were designed and it is the proper function for our spiritual doors and windows. It is good to open our heart to God. An example of this is Christian salvation; this is letting Jesus into our heart. Another example is the Baptism in the Holy Spirit; this is letting the Holy Spirit come and reside within us.

Another example is receiving guidance; wise guidance comes from opening the avenues of access of the Father's guidance and direction. Access to our heart in examples like these is very good. It is important for our growth as a Christian, walking out a successful Christian life, and for having an effective prayer life.

By contrast, access through the doors and windows of our heart can have negative consequences. Access via these doors and windows of the heart by the Devil and his forces, is a source of great trouble and hardship. Far too often people have been open to problems because they have not closed their spiritual doors and windows leaving open access to forces of darkness and evil.

We can control our spiritual access to our heart, it is a choice. Open access to God allows us to walk with and fellowship with Him. If we do this on a consistent basis we can abide with Him and we can enjoy the benefits of this close relationship, the result of our good choice.

> *If you abide in Me, and My words abide in you, you will ask what you desire, and it shall be done for you. By this My Father is glorified, that you bear much fruit; so you will be My disciples. "As the Father loved Me, I also have loved you; abide in My love. If you keep My commandments, you will abide in My love, just as I have kept My Father's commandments and abide in His love.*
>
> JOHN 15:7-10 (NKJV)

The key to abiding is maintaining the access of Jesus to our heart and our heart to Him, like a vine and a branch. Maintenance of this relationship comes from abiding with God. A key to success here is keeping the Father's commandments. Keeping His commandments is a choice; just like opening a door or window.

Control of the access to your heart, begins with a close walk with God; you cannot abide from far away. Jesus came to purchase for us the right of entry to the Father, so we can draw near to Him. Nearness to the Father, nearness to His Word, and nearness to His Holy Spirit, keeps us from opening access to our heart to forces of spiritual darkness.

Daily we need to review our acceptance of the Father's invitation to abide with Him. With this examination we must see if there are hindrances keeping us from Him or openings for the forces of spiritual darkness. We also need to check our choices. Daily, moment-by-moment, we can and must make good choices concerning access to our heart.

No one would ask the Devil to come into their heart and wreak havoc. That would be foolish. However, too often we make poor choices and the cumulative effect is like having an open door policy for our heart. It is the little choices we make that get us in trouble. Success in life and effective prayer depends on making good choices and controlling the access to our heart.

If we are going to have success in prayer, we must walk close with God and make wise choices. We must not let hindrances keeping us from God. We must guard against opening the way for the Devil. He is looking for opportunities and opportune times to attack; we must not give him opening.

Let us Pray!

ARTICLE 14

THE WATER TROUGH

One of the places we lived when I was growing up was a retired farm. The barn and corral were still there and in decent shape, but no one farmed the land. The man who owned the land, kept a couple of horses there and he arranged for my dad to water and feed the horses every morning. Many mornings I would help my dad. We would turn on the water to fill the water trough and put feed out for the horses.

Even though the trough was very large, we had to refill it every day. The horses drank a lot of water. My dad explained to me that it was very important for the horses to have water every day, without it they would die. The water trough also had some small leaks and between what the horses drank and the leaks, we always had to add water every day to top it off. In the winter time it was even harder work because before we could fill the trough, we had to break the ice from the surface.

In a previous article entitled, *Do Not Doubt* [article 12 in this book], we studied a key to successful application of faith in prayer, not doubting in our heart. Jesus opened the way for great power and success in prayer; the requirement for walking that way is faith. Doubt, the enemy of faith, will keep us from the way. And if given an opportunity, it will destroy our power and limit our success.

> *So Jesus answered and said to them, "Have faith in God. For assuredly, I say to you, whoever says to this mountain, 'Be removed and be cast into the sea,' and does not doubt in his heart, but believes that those things he says will be done, he will have whatever he says. Therefore I say to you, whatever things you ask when you pray, believe that you receive them, and you will have them. "And whenever you stand praying, if you have anything against anyone, forgive him, that your Father in heaven may also forgive you your trespasses. But if you do not forgive, neither will your Father in heaven forgive your trespasses."*
>
> MARK 11:22-26 (NKJV)

In another article, *Windows and Doors*, [article 13 in this book], we reviewed a few key verses concerning the protection of our heart from things like doubt. Chief among these is our dealing with the Word of God. If we are wise concerning this key we can enjoy the abundant life Jesus promised. Following the guidance of the Word of God also provides the basis for success in prayer.

> *My son, give attention to my words; Incline your ear to my sayings. Do not let them depart from your eyes; Keep them in the midst of your heart; For they are life to those who find them, And health to all their flesh. Keep your heart with all diligence, For out of it spring the issues of life. Put away from you a deceitful mouth, And put perverse lips far from you. Let your eyes look straight ahead, And your eyelids look right before you. Ponder the path of your feet,*

*And let all your ways be established. Do not turn to the
right or the left; Remove your foot from evil.*

PROVERBS 4:20-27 (NKJV)

Remember the water trough I told you about? Our heart is
like that water trough and the water we put in is the Word of
God. We need the Word and we must fill our heart every day.
We cannot fill our heart on Sundays and then expect to make
it successfully through the week. We must have the Word of
God and we need a daily infilling because of our consumption
of the Word, leakage, and hardening of our heart.

The Word of God is an essential ingredient to life. Just as
the water was required for the horses we fed, so we must feed
on God's Word. Every day we must refill our heart. The horses
would drink the water they needed for that day, but they
could not store up enough water to meet tomorrow's needs.
Tomorrow they would once again need to drink the water. We
must emulate their actions; every day we must drink deeply of
the Word of God and fill our heart. The Word of God is the
nourishment for our life and our ministry of prayer. If we are
going to have success in prayer, a filling of the Word is a must
and it must be a daily activity.

*But Jesus answered him, saying, "It is written, 'Man shall
not live by bread alone, but by every word of God."*

LUKE 4:4 (NKJV)

*Therefore, laying aside all malice, all deceit, hypocrisy,
envy, and all evil speaking, as newborn babes, desire
the pure milk of the word, that you may grow thereby, if
indeed you have tasted that the Lord is gracious.*

I PETER 2:1-3 (NKJV)

A daily filling is important and I do not want to shock you,
but we leak. I wish it was not so, and it should not be so, but

it is a fact, we leak. What is leaking out of our heart is the Word of God. I just stated that we need to refill the Word in our heart every day. One reason we need constant refilling is leakage. The world and its concerns cause people to leak the Word of God. We are constantly and powerfully bombarded by the world and its sin, concerns, and problems. These are like bullets piercing our heart, and this bombardment causes us to leak.

We are called to live in the world, but not of the world. Unfortunately we do not live everyday with our armor in place. We let down our guard and get pierced by the issues of life and death. The fiery darts of the wicked and the attack of evil around us, cause a drain of the Word in us. So once again, day-by-day, we must refill our heart with the Word of God.

> *For we do not wrestle against flesh and blood, but against principalities, against powers, against the rulers of the darkness of this age, against spiritual hosts of wickedness in the heavenly places. Therefore take up the whole armor of God, that you may be able to withstand in the evil day, and having done all, to stand. Stand therefore, having girded your waist with truth, having put on the breastplate of righteousness, and having shod your feet with the preparation of the gospel of peace; above all, taking the shield of faith with which you will be able to quench all the fiery darts of the wicked one. And take the helmet of salvation, and the sword of the Spirit, which is the word of God; praying always with all prayer and supplication in the Spirit, being watchful to this end with all perseverance and supplication for all the saints--*

EPHESIANS 6:12-18 (NKJV)

In spiritual things it is sometimes winter even in the summer. In the winter time when dad and I fed the horses there were times when the water would freeze and although the water line was near the top, the horses could not drink. The icy cap would keep them from the water. We run into this same situation with the Word of God in our heart. Even if our heart is full, we can be restricted from enjoying the benefit of the Word. It is like an icy cap over our heart.

What causes this icy cap to our heart? Cold weather froze the water creating an icy cap, in spiritual matters things like fear, anger, and unforgiveness create an icy cap. Our attitude makes a difference. The man who tries to have faith by filling his heart with the Word of God, but is overwhelmed by fear has an icy cap over his heart. The Word of God can melt this icy cap, but until it does, this man will be constrained in his faith. Unforgiveness freezes faith, stopping the hand of God. Anger and rage block the flow of faith. Anger is a simmering fire and rage is an uncontrolled inferno, but both, just like the icy cap on the horse trough, block the flow of faith. All of these can place a cap on faith and hinder the working of the Word of God in our heart.

Every day dad and I would have to chip away the ice that blocked the water from the horses. In much the same way we must chip away at fear, anger, unforgiveness and other sins that would block the flow of faith. At any cost we must not allow them to have a place in our heart.

Faith in prayer comes from keeping our heart filled with the Word and protecting our heart so we can enjoy the blessings and benefits of the Word. It is a daily battle; we must refill our heart everyday with the Word of God. We consume far too much of the world with daily living to be able to get by for several days without refilling. As long as we live in the world, we will need to refill our heart, we must refill because we leak. We must also chip away at fear, anger, unforgiveness, and other sins that come to hinder us. We must deal with them when they come; better yet, is not to let them come at all. Repudiate any entrance to fear. Refuse a place for anger. Forgive, so unforgiveness will have no place in your heart. Keep your heart; keep it filled with the Word of God, and keep access to your heart cleared for the unrestrained working of the Word of God in your life.

Let us Pray!

WILL

There is a story told about a little boy having breakfast with his father. You may have heard this story or a version of it, but it is a great story to help illustration our article today. In this story the little boy is standing in his chair. His father has fixed him a bowl of cereal and he wants the boy to sit down and eat. The little boy says, "No, I will not sit down". The father repeats his command, "Sit down." The little boy again refuses. The father, in his commanding voice says, "Sit down!!!!!!" The little boy sits down, but says, "I may be sitting down on the outside, but I am still standing on the inside."

One of the keys to success in prayer is dealing with our will and the many related problems. One problem that often hinders prayer is a lack of will to pray. Too often people do not make prayer a high priority and are casual about continuing in prayer, if they do pray. For these and many other reasons people, by their lack of will, do not pray or fail to be effective in prayer.

The man or woman who wants to be powerful in prayer must make wise choices of the will. They choose by their will to make what they are asking for a reality and not just a wish. It is a choice of, I will pray. I will make time to pray. I will read and study my Bible to build my faith. I will be faithful and believe God in prayer. These and other choices of our will are important ingredients in a recipe for success in prayer. Without a strong will to do things and to do them God's way, we will not pray effective prayers. We must set our will to hear, believe, and do what God commands.

As important a key as this is to successful prayer; this is not what I want to look at in this article. For effective prayer we must deal with the problem of our will; we also must deal with the conflict between our will and God's will. From the time of The Fall in the Garden, men have been rebellious; seeking to run their life, as they please. The battle of wills is one of the most fundamental struggles in life and prayer.

Examples of this struggle are seen in two experiences in gardens. In the Garden of Eden, Adam was told not to eat from the tree of the knowledge of good and evil, this was God's will. This became the temptation of Adam. In the Garden of Gethsemane, as Jesus prayed, the question of will came up. No sane man would want to go to the cross, especially if they knew what to expect, as Jesus did, (it was spelled out in many prophecies of the Bible). This was the final temptation for Jesus. In the Garden of Eden, Adam chooses his will over God's will. In the Garden of Gethsemane, Jesus chooses God's will over His own.

> *And He took Peter, James, and John with Him, and He began to be troubled and deeply distressed. Then He said to them, "My soul is exceedingly sorrowful, even to death. Stay here and watch." He went a little farther, and fell on the ground, and prayed that if it were possible, the hour*

might pass from Him. And He said, "Abba, Father, all things are possible for You. Take this cup away from Me; nevertheless, not what I will, but what You will."

MARK 14:33-36 (NKJV)

We face this same struggle, the battle of our will. As long as we choose our will over God's will, we limit and hinder all we do. However, we can and should win this battle and to win, we must yield our will to God's will. When we are Born Again we can yield to God's will because we are a new creation in Christ.

Therefore, if anyone is in Christ, he is a new creation; old things have passed away; behold, all things have become new.

2 CORINTHIANS 5:17 (NKJV)

A new creation has a new life. This new life is in Christ Jesus and one of the new things is obedience to God and His will. However, the flesh does not know it is not still in control. It continues to attempt to promote mutiny; taking every opportunity to bring rebellion. It tries to assert personal will over the will of God. In this struggle with the flesh, Jesus battled and won; we must do the same. Will our will rule over God's will or will we yield to His will? To win this battle Jesus willingly went to the cross. He was obedient to God's will. We must go to the cross as well.

I have been crucified with Christ; it is no longer I who live, but Christ lives in me; and the life which I now live in the flesh I live by faith in the Son of God, who loved me and gave Himself for me.

GALATIANS 2:20 (NKJV)

Crucified with Christ is the first step in this battle. Without this, the battle of the wills is lost. With this, the will of God can and should be victorious. However, everyday the flesh will try again to take control and periodically the Devil will come to tempt us. We must present our bodies as living sacrifices to God, and a key and basic part of this is submitting our will to God's will.

> *I beseech you therefore, brethren, by the mercies of God, that you present your bodies a living sacrifice, holy, acceptable to God, which is your reasonable service. And do not be conformed to this world, but be transformed by the renewing of your mind, that you may prove what is that good and acceptable and perfect will of God.*
>
> ROMANS 12:1-2 (NKJV)

The battle of wills is a key to success. Today, it is a well hidden secret for most people; there are so many other more glamorous things to talk about and do. This is why much of what we try to do is weak and ineffective. The anointed power of prayer comes to the man or woman yielded to and praying the will of God. This is what is desperately needed by the Body of Christ. Will you join with Jesus and declare, "Not my will, but Your will be done".

> *Now this is the confidence that we have in Him, that if we ask anything according to His will, He hears us. And if we know that He hears us, whatever we ask, we know that we have the petitions that we have asked of Him.*
>
> I JOHN 5:14-15 (NKJV)

Let us Pray!

ENDURANCE

My mother is a runner. She began running more than 25 years ago. She has won many races and has a wall full of medals. She continues to run, but does not train for or run marathons, at this time. When she ran marathons, part of her training régime was building her endurance. It is one thing to be able to compete at a high level for a short time or even for a longer race, but it is another thing to be at a high level for more than 26 miles.

To prepare for marathons she would do a lot of training. She would workout several times a week doing specific exercises geared toward building greater and greater endurance. When she ran a marathon, the race was very hard work, but because of all her training she was able to be successful and run with endurance.

The Christian life is filled with areas where it is important to be able to run with endurance. Chief among these is prayer. Effective prayer requires endurance.

For you have need of endurance, so that after you have
done the will of God, you may receive the promise:

This verse in Hebrews gives us some insight into the need for endurance. Please note that endurance comes after we have done the will of God. We must first do those things He requires of us, then, we can endure. We must do the believing in Jesus, the walking in faith, the asking according to His will, not doubting, and all the rest of what we have learned about effective prayer. After we have done these things then comes endurance. And if we are going to receive the promise we must endure. If we are talking about prayer, and I always am, then receiving the promise is receiving answers to prayer.

Then they said to Him, "What shall we do, that we may
work the works of God?" Jesus answered and said to them,
"This is the work of God, that you believe in Him whom
He sent."

JOHN 6:28-29 (NKJV)

And now, Israel, what does the Lord your God require
of you, but to fear the Lord your God, to walk in all
His ways and to love Him, to serve the Lord your God
with all your heart and with all your soul, and to keep
the commandments of the Lord and His statutes which I
command you today for your good?

DEUTERONOMY 10:12-13 (NKJV)

I like the word endurance better than patience, which is the word used in the King James Version in Hebrews 10:36, and either English word would fit the definition of the Greek word used in this passage. However, in modern usage both words have a poor connotation for our understanding of what we are to be doing based on this verse. They both give the idea of just waiting. They imply the idea of, now that we have done the required things, we can now just hang on until something happens. This is not the best way to think of this word. Our endurance is to be active and aggressive.

When my mom was preparing to run marathons, there where specific exercises and routines she would follow. She did more of the things she had been doing, such as running, both more often and longer distances. She also did many other exercises to prepare her body for the effort needed to run that far. She had to train her body to exchange oxygen better, to pump blood better, to burn energy more efficiently, and to deal with pain effectively. She had to move up to a higher plain for a runner.

In building an effective prayer life there are exercises and routines that we should follow to pray with endurance. In several places the Bible speaks of running a race and running to win. So we should be preparing for a race that we win in prayer. Endurance is like preparing for a marathon; it is doing the things we should be doing every day, but doing more of them and doing them better.

> *Do you not know that those who run in a race all run, but one receives the prize? Run in such a way that you may obtain it. And everyone who competes for the prize is temperate in all things. Now they do it to obtain a perishable crown, but we for an imperishable crown. Therefore I run thus: not with uncertainty. Thus I fight: not as one who beats the air. But I discipline my body and bring it into subjection, lest, when I have preached to others, I myself should become disqualified.*
>
> I CORINTHIANS 9:24-27 (NKJV)

Everything in effective prayer is by faith and faith comes by the Word of God. So our endurance training should include reading, listening to, memorizing, studying, and meditating on the Word of God. There are other keys to faithful prayer; for example, we must forgive, we must not doubt, we must lay aside every problem and hindrance, and so forth. All this and more is needed to build up to the challenge of enduring.

> *Therefore we also, since we are surrounded by so great a cloud of witnesses, let us lay aside every weight, and the sin which so easily ensnares us, and let us run with endurance the race that is set before us,*
>
> HEBREWS 12:1 (NKJV)

> *My brethren, count it all joy when you fall into various trials, knowing that the testing of your faith produces patience. But let patience have its perfect work, that you may be perfect and complete, lacking nothing. If any of you lacks wisdom, let him ask of God, who gives to all liberally and without reproach, and it will be given to him. But let him ask in faith, with no doubting, for he who doubts is like a wave of the sea driven and tossed by the wind. For let not that man suppose that he will receive anything from the Lord; he is a double-minded man, unstable in all his ways.*
>
> JAMES 1:2-8 (NKJV)

Endurance in prayer is stepping up toward the high standard set by Jesus, the champion of prayer. He did everything commanded by the Bible and was the perfect man in action, faith, and prayer. The question is what about us? Will we avail ourselves of the training of the Holy Spirit, doing the exercises and work required to endure in prayer? Will we give of our life, time, and effort to pray at a higher level and for as long as it takes? It is time for endurance training for effective prayer.

Let us Pray!

MAKING A FAITHFUL STAND

In 1786 a group of men met together in Philadelphia, their charge, make changes to the Articles of Confederation, the constitution of America at that time. It was obvious that there needed to be some change; the Articles were inadequate for meeting the needs of the fledgling nation. In a bold move the delegates chose not to modify, but to write a completely new constitution.

However, very quickly the convention became embroiled in conflict. The record kept by James Madison indicates the convention was on the verge of dissolving without writing anything. Faction was against faction, with the battles growing more and more heated. At this point in the proceedings Benjamin Franklin made a speech. He recalled that when the Continental Congress sat during a time of great danger, they had asked God's help in prayer.

"Have we forgotten our powerful Friend? Or do we imagine we no longer need its assistance?" "And the longer I live the more convincing proofs I see of this truth, that God governs in the affairs of men. And if a sparrow cannot fall to the ground without his notice, is it probable that an empire can rise without his aid?" He then quoted the Bible, "Except the Lord build the house, they labor in vain that build it."

Following the words of Franklin, attitudes at the convention changed and the delegates began to work together to develop the American Constitution. They were within days, maybe hours, of the convention falling apart and then suddenly they were able to write the most extraordinary document, ever written by man, governing the affairs of man. What happened, they remembered God. They included Him in their efforts. It would be good for us, as men and women of prayer, to remember some of Franklin's words, "…is it probable that an empire can rise without His aid?"

These words are just as true today, as they were then, empires come and go, but these comings and goings never surprise God. He has His hand in the rise and fall of nations now just as He did in the times recorded in the Bible. Men and women of prayer should be aware, that God works with nations. And it is noteworthy, that He has arranged for prayer to move His hand. History records an extraordinary number of times people have prayed and God has answered. God's response to prayer has turned the course of nations, changed the flow of battles, overthrown kings and kingdoms, defeated powerful foes, and overcome seemingly impossible odds.

With this wonderful record of God's response to prayer, what is our response to His call for prayer? Are we like those who do not pray? Are we barricaded away, praying, but just watching the world as it goes waltzing by, never seeking or receiving answers to prayers? Or are we like those delegates who responded to Franklin's words and worked through the problems? Will we work through our problems? Will we come to the point where God can work with us and thru us? Will we work with the Holy Spirit, learning to pray, so the changes the world so desperately needs come today?

The situation we are in is different from that of the delegates, they had to hammer out a plan of government, we must pray for people and nations. However, the call is similar in that both, the constitutional delegates and men and women of prayer, must call on God, if they are to be successful. There is no other way.

We must pray for help today; people and nations are without God; the times are desperate. Nations are making plans, effective, fervent prayers that avail much, will make the difference in those plans and their actions. People are desperate, without hope or direction; prayer prepares hearts and minds for hearing and receiving hope from the good news of the Gospel. Today is desperate for prayer!

We need to pray. Is it probable that nations will do the right things without His aid? Is it probable that revival can come without His aid? Is it probable that men and women can be saved without His aid?

Let us Pray!

The articles of this Unit explore the nature and practices of men and women of effective, fervent prayer that avails much. These articles are presented to help people make a faithful stand in prayer.

ARTICLE 17

FIRST

Do you remember the first time when you saw...? When I was stationed in Germany my parents came to visit. For two weeks we traveled around Europe and we saw great castles, rivers, and cities. One of many special places we saw was Zermatt, Switzerland. While on the train I described to my folks the beauty of the Matterhorn as it looks over the valley below. I also cautioned that many times people have come to see the mountain, only to find it shrouded by clouds. However, my caution was not needed, when we arrived the grand mountain was at its best. The sky was cloudless and the Matterhorn seemed to lean out over the valley to greet us. I will never forget that first time my parents saw the Matterhorn.

You have many first in your life as well. The first time you saw, did, or said things. These can be great memories and sometimes, times you would like to forget. There are firsts of many kinds in life, including firsts in prayer. While most of us may not remember it, there was a first time we prayed. There is the first time we prayed and saw God distinctly answer our prayer. In addition to first like this, Paul tells us to make prayer first.

Paul, the great man of prayer, in his letter to Timothy, exhorted that the first thing is to pray. He exhorted. Now I do not know about you, but I do not use the word exhort very often. So just to be wise I thought I should review the definition. Exhort means to incite by argument or advice, to urge strongly, to give warnings or advice, to make an urgent appeal. That seems to say that Paul feels strongly about this subject. He is giving his young follower an important piece of advice. He is warning Timothy about something significant and of great consequence. He thinks it is or should be an essential part of Timothy's life. If this was that important for Timothy, then how important is it for us? This must be something that is crucial for us to read carefully, think deeply about, and take wise action upon.

> *Therefore I exhort first of all that supplications, prayers,*
> *intercessions, and giving of thanks be made for all men,*
> *for kings and all who are in authority, that we may lead a*
> *quiet and peaceable life in all godliness and reverence.*
> I TIMOTHY 2:1-2 (NKJV)

Paul exhorts Timothy, first of all, pray! This is a very powerful and important advice. Unfortunately most people are in such a rush, when they read these verses, to get to the kings and authorities, to the quiet and peaceable life, and to all godliness and reverence. They often miss the key point of the exhortation. First Pray!

It is important that we pray for kings and authorities, but we must not miss the primary point. First pray! What does this mean, first pray! I like to keep it simple and take the meaning of the words as just what they say and we know that in our interpretations of verses of scripture, we must stay within the guidance of the overall writing of the Bible, so the meaning of these words seems very simple, the first thing we should do is pray. It does not say the only thing, , but it does say the first thing is to pray.

There are many keys to success in prayer; faith, faithfulness, forgiveness, a pure heart and motive, and so many others. Paul in his prayers brings attention to another key. Look at an example in Paul's prayer recorded in Romans chapter 1; he begins by saying, "First".

> *First, I thank my God through Jesus Christ for you all,*
> *that your faith is spoken of throughout the whole world.*
> ROMANS 1:8 (NKJV)

The word translated, "first", in this prayer means, firstly in time, place, order, or importance. Paul knew and demonstrated over and over again that prayer needs to be first in our spiritual life and wellbeing. The Christian life, well lived, daily begins with prayer and continues in prayer moment-by-moment. Paul also knew that prayer was of chief importance for success, so it must be given a place of great importance in our daily living. Very simply, the initial key to success in this verse is, first we should pray. The second key is to give prayer its rightful place, the place of primacy over all else, in importance in our life.

Whenever we do anything, we should pray first. When we go to the grocery store we should pray first. We should pray that there will be the items we need for our family. We should pray that we will get great price and value for the things we buy. We should pray that we will be wise in our buying, getting the things we really need. We should pray that we will have opportunities to share the Gospel with people we meet. We should pray for safety coming and going to the store. And still there are more things we should pray about on this trip to the store, but Paul's exhortation is that we should pray first. Too often we get home and think about what we should have bought, done, or said. Praying first is a key to seizing the moment.

What about when we go to work, we should pray first. Pray first for safe travel, for having a job, for success in our work and for the company. For good relations with the people we work with and work for. If more people prayed first for their employers before they went to work there would be more successful businesses. In a time of economic down turn it is the prayers of people that make a difference for companies surviving. God is the source of blessing for that company and it comes through prayer, and Paul, via Timothy, exhorts you to pray first. Pray first for every aspect of your job and the business. Far too often we work hard, but we are not as successful as we should be. The answer is; pray first.

When we go to church, what is the first thing you do? Do you take time and pray? Too many people just go to church. They do not pray first for the service, the ministers, for the other people, for the lost to come to the service, for opportunities for the Gospel to be preached, taught, shared and received. We need to be praying for our church, church family, church ministry, church outreaches, church health and welfare, for our church finances, and so much more. Pray first!

I hope you are seeing Paul's point here, in everything we do and say, we should pray first. Some people might say they do not have time for this. I counter with asking you to think of all the time you spend fixing problems and mistakes. Save time, pray first! This does not have to take much time, it is not by the length of your prayer or by the fancy words you use, that your prayers are heard, it is by faith. Some of the most powerful prayers of Jesus were very short and to the point.

Now when He had said these things, He cried with a loud voice, "Lazarus, come forth!"

JOHN 11:43 (NKJV)

This powerful prayer, but it is also a very short prayer. Please do not tell me that you do not have time for a quick prayer like this. Even a few prayers, filled with faith, prayed first, will save you a great deal of time and trouble. Pray first! And please note this was a prayer. Read the verses just before this verse and note the results of this prayer.

Then they took away the stone from the place where the dead man was lying. And Jesus lifted up His eyes and said, "Father, I thank You that You have heard Me. And I know that You always hear Me, but because of the people who are standing by I said this, that they may believe that You sent Me." Now when He had said these things, He cried with a loud voice, "Lazarus, come forth!" And he who had died came out bound hand and foot with graveclothes, and his face was wrapped with a cloth. Jesus said to them, "Loose him, and let him go."

JOHN 11:41-44 (NKJV)

If we want to be faithful in prayer, we must pray first. If we want to learn to be successful in prayer, we must pray first. If we want to have power in prayer, we must pray first!

We are called to pray. This is a great privileged and opportunity given by God to his children. The God of the universe has made provision so you and I may come to Him in prayer. We can come boldly before His throne and pray. How can we resist such an opportunity? One of the keys to success in prayer is to pray first.

Again I say to you that if two of you agree on earth concerning anything that they ask, it will be done for them by My Father in heaven.

MATTHEW 18:19 (NKJV)

Now this is the confidence that we have in Him, that if we ask anything according to His will, He hears us. And if we know that He hears us, whatever we ask, we know that we have the petitions that we have asked of Him.

I JOHN 5:14-15 (NKJV)

Let us Pray!

SUCCESS IN PRAYER

For many years I coached football (American football) and one year we did not have a very good team. We had a few good young men, but just not enough. One day the head coach and I sat in the commons area of the school and watched as good athlete after good athlete walked past. Many of these athletes did not play football. We counted and there were more good athletes not playing compared to the good athletes who were playing. We began to talk to some of these young men. We asked them questions concerning why they did not play football. There were many answers, but one of the most common was fear of failure. These young men would not take a chance of making mistakes and looking bad. The result was, since there were not enough risk takers; we had a horrible season, winning only one game.

Great men and women of prayer are risk takers. Too often our prayers are just general prayers of unknown value. We pray for the things we need, the things that are part of every day life. We pray for daily bread, but we trust that our supply of the bread will come from the store. We pray for someone to get better from a sickness or disease, but we trust in the remedies prescribed by the doctor to do the trick sooner or later. It is easy to pray general prayers, we do not risk failure, there never is a concern about responsibility for the answer or the lack there of.

Many people are content to pray knowing as long as it is just an exercise, they need not be concerned if answers come or not. They believe the results of prayer are in the hand of God and use this as a copout. In reality their results are poor due to a lack of faith in prayer. People are not concerned with the results, because they have no expectation of answers. They do not believe the results have anything to do with them. Prayer for these people is the ultimate, "what ever will be will be".

This is very freeing; when I am not responsible for what happens I am not troubled. However, this leaves the power of prayer in the can. It is like baking soda. The power of baking soda, used in baking, is nothing in the can, it is only when it is placed in the mix that it begins to work, and it then releases its power. The same is true for prayer, when we leave prayer in the can, there is no power. However, we know there is power in prayer and by faith we can take prayer out of the can. We can release God's power to work, expecting answers from Him.

There are many reasons for lack in this area; fear of course is a key. If I begin to pray with a responsibility for the results, then I might fail. Just like those young men who would not play football, the fear of failure keeps many prayers left unprayed.

I called on the Lord in distress; The Lord answered me and set me in a broad place. The Lord is on my side; I will not fear. What can man do to me?

PSALM 118:5-6 (NKJV)

The fear of failure has become so ingrained in our thinking that most people only do things they know they will do well. In schools, I see students unwilling to take classes where there is a possibility of failure, many will not take a class if there is even a chance of anything less that a top score. In prayer, we see the same thing; people will not pray for healing or deliverance, if they do, they must face the possibility of failure. Fear demands not taking a chance.

However, extraordinary prayer is different. It is faith, faith that will take risks, that makes it extraordinary and powerful. Extraordinary prayer believes God answers prayer and requires faith. It takes the chance of failure, to gain the opportunity for success.

> *But without faith it is impossible to please Him, for he who comes to God must believe that He is, and that He is a rewarder of those who diligently seek Him. By faith Noah, being divinely warned of things not yet seen, moved with godly fear, prepared an ark for the saving of his household, by which he condemned the world and became heir of the righteousness which is according to faith.*
>
> HEBREWS 11:6-7 (NKJV)

The great men and women of prayer have always been great risk takers. They put their faith to the test. They often pray boldly for people, and as a result people know about their prayers and see the results. If they fail, everyone knows. This could be a fearful thing; however they are daring and allow God to work. This boldness of faith takes responsibility and action. It prays the prayers that cannot be prayed any other way. It is risky, but it should be the norm for Christians. And it brings great results.

If you were to die today, could they make your epitaph, "Bold in Faith and Prayer"? Take responsibility; be bold in prayer, confident in the power and ability of God to do what He has said He will do. It is His power and might that will carry the day, and carry your prayers to answers. It takes the chance of failure, to gain the opportunity for success.

Let us Pray!

ARTICLE 19

GOD ANSWERS PRAYER

L ife is filled with tests. Tests are common in education, and life; the Bible is full of them. Book after book in the Bible is a record of people and the tests they faced. Some people passed and some failed. In the Bible the tests are the kind common to most people today. The details of each test may vary slightly, but the fundamentals of the tests are the same.

Look at a few of the more famous tests. For example, there was Adam and Eve in the garden. What was the test? It was obedience, God had told them not to eat of that one tree. The result of that test was not good, eating was not obeying. Take a look at Peter and stepping out of the boat. What was the test? It was faith. The result of the test was mixed. He did well as long as he kept his eyes on Jesus and he sank into the water when he looked at the waves. Another test, the Hebrew spies. What was the test? It was a test of believing in the power and promises of God. The result was bad for all, except for the two, Caleb and Joshua, who passed this test; they were ready to take the Promised Land.

A test tells a story. In education tests are designed to tell the story of student progress, how the mind and the abilities of the student have matured and developed. If a student is not prepared, a test can be scary; however for the prepared student a test reveals his or her learning. A test can be valuable for revealing areas of shortfall and mastery. What is revealed by testing can be a valuable tool in every aspect of life, including prayer.

A prayer test can be very valuable. There are many areas of prayer that can be explored. Here is an example of a prayer test; this test focuses on beliefs and prayer. As you look at each question, with the help of the Holy Spirit, check to see if you fully, continually, and faithfully believe. The Holy Spirit will reveal shortfalls, and encourage the growth and maturity necessary to be effective in prayer. If He reveals areas that need work, if He reveals doubt, fear, or sin; repent. Let the Word of God and the blood of the Lamb wash you clean. Let the fire of the Holy Spirit burn out any impurities in your life. The Holy Spirit, our teacher, is here to help us grow strong in faith and powerful in prayer, so let Him work.

So, here is a little test.

Question One
Do you believe God answers prayers?

This is a simple question, not intended to doubt your beliefs, but to encourage you to check and make sure you are in the faith in this area. It is so easy to give lip service to our beliefs, and to slip into doubt. For this self-exam, ask the Holy Spirit to help. If you ask, He will reveal your heart, so you and He might rejoice in your faith or deal with your lack of faith.

Question Two

Do you believe it is by grace God answers prayer?

In other words have you come to the point where you know the answers to prayer are in no way by your strength, ability, or position? Israel got into trouble because they thought their position, as God's chosen people gave them special position. With this position they thought He would answer even if they did not serve Him properly. God answers, not by position, but by grace. Today many people still fall into this trap. They expect answers because they trust in their going to church, doing good works, or other things; however there is no position good enough to, in effect, earn an answer from God. It is true, even as it was in the time of Paul, "all have sinned and fall short of the glory of God", Romans 3:23 (NKJV) and if answers depend on our ability or goodness, then there will be no answers. So, Praise God it is by grace He answers prayer!

Question Three

Do you believe God answers prayer, sometimes answering immediately?

God is amazing, sometimes He answers so quickly it takes our breath away. We pray and before we can finish we have the answer! Wow, we love this and know that a prayer life is great! However, immediate prayer can have dangers. It is very easy to fall in to the snare of the enemy even here and view immediate answers to prayer as a measuring rod of our spirituality. It is an error to think, "If I get quick answers, I must be spiritual". This is deception and can be very dangerous.

Many people, especially ministers, regularly face this test question. The problem is that it is easy to think, "If there are many people coming to church, so I must be good". Many of the ministries that have fallen into sin have fallen in this way. "My ministry is saving many, so God approves of what I am doing, even if I am living in sin". This is claiming that God winks at my sin. Oh, what a stumbling block success can be. And just a note, it may seem strange, but the opposite can be a problem as well. Men often think; if the church numbers are not going up, it proves that the minister is not a good minister. This is not correct either.

While this question is especially important for ministers, it applies to all Christians and is a very important question for men and women of prayer. God answers prayer; He asks us to pray and He delights to answer. However, His answers are not a vindication of our life or lifestyle. His answers are answers to prayer. His answers are by grace.

Question Four

Do you believe God answers prayer, sometimes after a delay?

Prayer and delay is a difficult issue. Many people have lost their faith in prayer, due to delay. God answers prayer, but when the answer tarries, it is hard to stay away from doubt, fear, and other concerns. The enemy is very willing to whisper in your ear and try to destroy your confidence in God. However, if we are going to be successful in prayer, we must remain faithful, even when the answer seems slow in coming.

> *Let us hold fast the confession of our hope without wavering, for He who promised is faithful.*
>
> HEBREWS 10:23 (NKJV)

> *Therefore do not cast away your confidence, which has great reward. For you have need of endurance, so that after you have done the will of God, you may receive the promise:*
>
> HEBREWS 10:35-36 (NKJV)

It is easy to have questions when the answer is delayed. We improperly do and say many things because we are too close to the need to have any perspective. However, God knows the correct timing for answers. He is never late. How often have we yielded to the pressure of the time, to the whisper of the enemy, or to the heaviness of the need, only to have given up just before the answer comes? Paul knew about this, his command, "…having done all, to stand. Stand therefore".

> *Therefore take up the whole armor of God, that you may be able to withstand in the evil day, and having done all, to stand. Stand therefore, having girded your waist with truth, having put on the breastplate of righteousness,*
>
> EPHESIANS 6:13-14 (NKJV)

Question Five

Do you believe God answers your prayer, even if the answer is different from your desire?

God answers prayers and sometimes the answer is different from what we desire. I think I know what I want, but I do not always know what is best. As parents, we know this. I like ice cream, and since man does not live by bread alone, he must live by ice cream. So, "Anytime, anywhere, ice cream for me", is my prayer. However, I know this is not a good prayer for God to answer (I would weight 400 pounds). But, often when we pray, we are like a spoiled child wanting ice cream. We throw a temper tantrum, kick and scream, if we do not get what we want. But, Father knows best.

Some would claim; see, God knows best and so sometimes He does not answer prayer. Once again as parents, we know the answer to this concern. If my children knew what was good for them, they would ask correctly. Our Father knows what is best for us and He has sent His Word (the Bible) and the Holy

Spirit to instruct us on prayer and guide us on what to pray. By the guidance of the Word and the Holy Spirit, my prayer is not for ice cream, but for my daily bread, (what I need for good nutrition and some fun). When we pray by the guidance of the Holy Spirit, we pray the prayers of the Father. We pray with understanding and wisdom. Jesus prayed what He heard the Father say. We should pray what the Father, Son, and Holy Spirit say to pray.

Question Six

Do you believe God answers prayer and sometimes goes beyond our expectation?

Do your prayers limit God? A few years ago, my wife had health concerns and the doctors determined she had to have surgery. The surgery was very successful and she is doing well. Many people prayed for her, people from many churches and groups, from several countries. Before the surgery, a well-meaning person said, "Thank God for surgeons". And then said, "Often surgery is God's best". I mumbled something and went on, but this was like a slap in the face. Nothing against this person and I am thankful that there are surgeons, but Jesus did not send the woman with the issue of blood to another doctor. He did not send the man with the withered hand to the doctor. Healing was God's best.

When we pray how often do we limit God, how often do we restrict Him from giving His best? How often do we accept less than what God has planned for us? How often do we limit God by our low expectations?

> *Call to Me, and I will answer you, and show you great and mighty things, which you do not know.*
>
> JEREMIAH 33:3 (NKJV)

*Now to Him who is able to do exceedingly abundantly
above all that we ask or think, according to the power that
works in us,*

EPHESIANS 3:20 (NKJV)

How did you do with the test? Are there areas where you need to work? Do not be condemned; tests are to help us see areas that we need to work on and areas where we need help. The Holy Spirit is our teacher, He will help us to learn and mature so we will pass the tests of life. Prayer by prayer we must believe, fully, continually, faithfully, and act in faith until we know God's answers prayer, and until we see His answers to prayer.

Let us Pray!

PRACTICE

The Berlin Wall was a symbol of the battle between East and West during the Cold War. For nearly all of the years that the Wall stood, most people believed that the Berlin Wall had become a permanent feature of the city. They believed that just like the castles that dot the countryside of Germany, that have been there for centuries, so the Wall would stand. There were ministries going into the East to reach people with the Gospel, but these efforts were restricted, it was difficult, and in many ways efforts were limited. What was needed was a radical change; the Wall needed to come down.

Most people saw the Wall as the way things would be, if not forever, at least for the foreseeable future. However, there were other people who believed in the power of God to answer even the seemingly impossible prayers. They believed that God could and would bring down the Wall, so they prayed. People prayed through the decades of the '60s, '70s, and '80s. God heard their prayers and moved to change Europe and the world; the Wall came down. That is long term praying and powerful prayer.

Long term prayer can be very powerful prayers and deserves to be explored. Long term prayer is a practice of praying beyond the immediate need of today and beyond quick prayer practices. In Isaiah 62 we read that God has set watchmen on the walls of Jerusalem. Their assignment is to never be quiet. They are to pray until God "makes Jerusalem a praise in the earth". Now this has not come to pass, yet. There are many places where Jerusalem is anything but well received and definitely not well thought of. Some people hate Jerusalem, at least when it is under the control of the Jews. The watchmen set on the walls have been praying for centuries, one generation after another. These prayers will be answered, but until then, prayers for Jerusalem must continue. This is long term prayer.

> *I have set watchmen on your walls, O Jerusalem; They shall never hold their peace day or night. You who make mention of the Lord, do not keep silent, And give Him no rest till He establishes And till He makes Jerusalem a praise in the earth.*
>
> ISAIAH 62:6-7 (NKJV)

Some of you have been a part of various long term prayers and have been for years (I know we have readers who prayed for the tearing down of the Berlin Wall). Many of you have begun to look beyond today with your prayers, looking beyond the needs of just your immediate family. Many of you are looking for help with your praying and looking for ways to bring more power and efficacy to your prayers. So perhaps it would be good to look at developing and improving our long term prayers. Many of the things that are helpful for long term prayer are good for prayers in general so this is a good study for all of us.

One of the keys to success in prayer is a careful look at our practices. Much of what is required for effective prayer is unnatural for most people. Few people are willing to change their normal way of living to become effective in prayer. They will pray, but only in their own chosen ways and at their chosen times. And for the most part they get poor results.

Because some of the demands of prayer are not the natural way we do things, we must make adjustments, if we are going to be successful. Change is not easy; this is why few people have great success in prayer; they will not make the alterations needed for success. Making changes takes great decisions and effort.

And from the days of John the Baptist until now the kingdom of heaven suffers violence, and the violent take it by force.

MATTHEW 11:12 (NKJV)

When Jesus was talking to the people about the life and ministry of John the Baptist, He makes a very interesting comment. Did you notice? He said, "The violent take it by force". The word translated violent in this statement means "a forcer". We could say, "The forcer takes it by force". If we are going to pray long term and if we are going to have effective prayer, we must force the issues.

The concept of forcing the issues seems a bit strange. It is not the type of thing often spoken of in conjunction with prayer. This is an unusual challenge, but one that we must respond to. If we take the normal route through life we will not be effective in prayer, nor will we continue on to long term prayer. So we must go beyond normal practices.

When I first began to coach football (American football), I met a very good coach; he knew many keys for helping boys be successful. One of the keys was attention to details at practices. He would drill the boys and make them do everything over and over. He explained that they had to drill until they would do things perfectly. They had to drill until they would do everything correctly even in the heat of battle in the game. Some things in football seem very strange, and the players often had to force themselves to do things correctly time after time.

In much the same way we must force ourselves to do things correctly in prayer. In some of what we do when we pray, both physical and spiritual things, we face going against what seems natural. Effective prayer makes demands on us. It will force change in our practices, when our practices are not effective.

For example, to be effective in prayer we need faith. Faith comes by the Word of God. We may need to make changes and then practice these changes, so that our heart will be full of the Word of God. We may need to read and study the Word. We may also need to make changes to what we say. It can be very difficult to put a watch over what comes from our mouth. However, if we do not study the Word and if we continue to say things that destroy our faith, we will not be successful in prayer.

It may take one or more good decisions, followed by days or even weeks of practice, to make the changes we want. We may have to force ourselves to change how we think or act, to come to the place where we can pray effectively. This can be difficult at times. We may have to believed God and what He says, even when the evidence is against us. Like Abraham, we can force belief in God and His abilities, even in the face of strong evidence against us.

> *And not being weak in faith, he did not consider his own*
> *body, already dead (since he was about a hundred years*

old), and the deadness of Sarah's womb. He did not waver at the promise of God through unbelief, but was strengthened in faith, giving glory to God, and being fully convinced that what He had promised He was also able to perform.

We have had the opportunity to read about good practices for effective prayer in the articles of *Voice of Thanksgiving*. Those practices are helpful, but they are not effective if they are not practiced. Often it takes force for us to make adjustments to our normal practices. Most people will not force the transformation. And even if we are willing to make these modifications, we must practice them over and over until they become ingrained in our thinking and life. We must practice them so we will continue to do them even in the heat of battle.

What changes does the Holy Spirit want you to make so you can and will pray effective prayers? We must force ourselves to make these changes. It may be a physical change, for instance in lifestyle. It may be a spiritual change, such as in what we say or do. It may be a change in what we believe, such as fully trusting in God's promises. Whatever changes we must make will take a force of effort, a force of mind, and a force of spirit. The life of men and women, who are effective in prayer, has many episodes of forcing change. And so must we.

Like those football players, we must practice doing things God's way and practice so we will do them His way every time. We must do what He says to do. We must live how He says we should live. We must believe how He says we should believe. We must say what He says we should say. We must pray how He says to pray.

What are you practicing today? What do you need to do to be successful in prayer? What do you need to force in your practices and beliefs so you can be effective? Will you force out the issues that keep you from receiving answers? Will you be bold and forceful like Jacob, demanding a blessing?

> *Then Jacob was left alone; and a Man wrestled with him until the breaking of day. Now when He saw that He did not prevail against him, He touched the socket of his hip; and the socket of Jacob's hip was out of joint as He wrestled with him. And He said, "Let Me go, for the day breaks." But he said, "I will not let You go unless You bless me!"*
>
> GENESIS 32:24-26 (NKJV)

Will you practice until you can and will say; I will not let you go unless you bless me!

Let us Pray!

ARTICLE 21

DELAY

The people who live across the street from us just had a son. This is their first child and everyone is doing well. It has been fun to watch as they have gotten very excited as the birth date drew near. There were all the preparations to make, changing a room into a nursery/bedroom, buying clothing and supplies for a newborn, and preparing to be parents. There was the picking of a name and telling parents and friends the impending good news. This couple even went through the process of a dry run for the birth, when they thought it was time for the grand appearance, only to find they had to wait a few more days. Finally the long awaited day arrived and everyone was pleased to see this boy.

From the earliest times to the present, the birth of a child has been a very special occasion. The birth of a child is one of the great joys of life. It is so special we celebrate this day every year with a birthday party. All births are special times however the Bible records some that were extra special. First to come to mind and best known is the birth of Jesus. Another very special birth was that of Isaac.

*For Sarah conceived and bore Abraham a son in his old
age, at the set time of which God had spoken to him.*

GENESIS 21:2 (NKJV)

The people across the street from us have been and are very
excited with the birth of their son, and well they should be.
However, can you imagine the excitement the birth of Isaac
was to parents, relatives, and friends? Few births have caused
such a stir to everyone who heard about it. When he finally
came, it was wonderful and exciting, but the waiting, year-after-year, and the struggle of dealing with the perceived delay
of God's answering His promise to give them a son, must have
been very difficult for Abraham and Sarah.

Delay is always difficult, and especially challenging when
dealing with a delay of answers to our prayers. Some people do
not know anything about what I am writing here; they never
experience delay in answers to prayer because their nebulous
prayers receive no answers and none are expected. If you do
not expect answers, you never experience delay. However, they
have never experience the thrill of an answer birthed in prayer.

If you have been praying for sometime and been expecting
to have answers to prayer, you have experienced dealing with
delay. There are times in our praying when God will do like
He did for Abraham and announce a set time for the answer.
However, often God does not tell us of His time schedule or
His plans. There is an expectation in faith that we will trust
God's power and might, and also His faithfulness. He expects
us to, by faith, know that He can and will answer. He also expects us to trust Him with the timing. Please note a key phrase
in the announcement of Isaac's birth, "at the set time". It would
be valuable for us to remember that God works at His set time
and there will be times this causes issues around perceived
delay.

The first point when dealing with delay, and most important, is to remember that God is never late. This is an easy thing for us to say, but in the heat of battle, when we have prayed long and hard, it is an opportune time for the enemy to whisper doubt in our ear. The Devil may tell us things like, God is busy, God is mad at us, we are not good enough to get an answer, or any of a myriad of explanations as to why answers are delayed. We must have a firm footing of absolute confidence that God is never late.

After we agree that God is never late, we still must deal with perceived delays. As we grow and mature in prayer, God will give us assignments in prayer. And often we will have to deal with the problem of perceived delay in the coming of the answer to our prayers. One cause of the problem is not listening to God and hearing His plan and timing. Think how hard it would have been for Abraham and Sarah if they had not heard from God the, "set time of which God had spoken to him", they had already waited a long time. Too often we are so excited, we do not listen and we do not hear God's timing. We are often guilty of assuming that things mean this or that, not having heard from God. And for most people anytime seems as good as another, so they think God should answer on their schedule, but God has His perfect timing and He does not waiver from His set times.

> *Then Jesus said to them, "My time has not yet come, but your time is always ready. The world cannot hate you, but it hates Me because I testify of it that its works are evil. You go up to this feast. I am not yet going up to this feast, for My time has not yet fully come."*
>
> JOHN 7:6-8 (NKJV)

There are times when God does not share with us, His planned timing. Faith is being able to believe God at His word and not have to see things before they happen. This includes having to have a time chart that spells out the timing of coming answers and events. Faith often demands walking with God and trusting in His faithfulness, no mater what we see or hear. It demands that we stand firm in faith believing, what He has said, He will do, even when it seems the answer is delayed.

We must settle firmly in our heart that we trust God. We must establish with out wavering that we will wait for God and trust His timing. We must prove that we will continue in faith and prayer until God says stop or the answer comes. This must be our faith statement and the action of our life. Most of the time this matter must be settled in our heart before the answer will come.

Another key to dealing with delay is dealing with maturing. Our Father is interested in more than just answers to prayer. He could bring the answer faster and easier other ways, but He wants us to grow and mature in prayer and in every aspect of Christian life.

One time when I was a boy, I went to visit my Grandparents and my Grandpa decided this would be a good time to build birdhouses. He was not interested in just building these houses or in having me watch him build them, he wanted me to learn how to use carpentry tools. It was much easier for him to build the houses and they would have been better, if he had built them. However, he believed that there comes a time when a boy needs to learn to build things and the birdhouses were a great project for these lessons. Slowly he took me through the process. We selected the wood and he taught me how to make a straight cut with a hand saw, and how to drive a nail straight and true. He taught me how to use a hand drill and to determine the correct bit to use for the right sized opening for the birds we wanted to attract. He taught me to paint and complete the project so the birdhouses would be useful and attractive. We built three houses and there were birds that made these houses their home every year as long as my Grandparents lived in their home.

God is looking for opportunities like this for us. It is important to Him that we learn the lessons of life and He uses every opportunity to teach us. One of the great values of prayer is that it can be a tool in God's hand for teaching His children. Please note that I wrote the words, it can be a great tool. Unfortunately some people refuse to allow God to work with them and the opportunities for lessons are lost. Personalized teaching, like the one-on-one method used by my Grandpa, is what God wants to give to you and me. As we learn our lessons, God takes us to the next opportunity.

Often what seems like a delay to us is just our lesson time. We may be learning to trust God more fully, how to deal with sin and hindrances, or any of the many other things God wants to teach us and perfect in our life. Please note Our Father longs for us to learn His lessons, but He does not force us to learn. I could have told my Grandpa, no, I do not want to learn how to make a birdhouse, it takes to long. Or I could have given up when I found I could not cut a board straight with a hand saw (that is until Grandpa taught me the secret). If I had stopped the opportunity, I would have missed the lessons and the learning. If we do not continue, even in what may seems like a delay, we will miss great lessons and opportunities to learn what God has prepared for us.

Delays in receiving answers to prayers can be very frustrating, but it is an opportunity for faith and trust. It can be an opportunity for lessons on the many issues of Christian life. The question is not what to do about delays, but if we will allow the seeming delay to be a time for instruction and testing. If we will faithfully walk with God and continue in His working in our life, He will take us through our lessons to the next place of maturity (at that place there awaits a new lesson). When we face delay we should seek Our Father and His lessons for our life, as we do, we will see that He answers, "At the set time".

Let us Pray!

FINISHING PRAYER

Jesus said to them, My food is to do the will of Him who sent Me, and to finish His work.

JOHN 4:34 (NKJV)

A local football team (American football) has a problem. They play well at the beginning of each game, but they do not do well in the second half. In several games they have been ahead or at least close to the score of the other team and then in the second half they lost the game. I am sure that you know of teams like this, in various sports. They are as good as the other teams, but they do not finish well and so they loose more than they should.

To begin to pray is very important, but if we are going to pray effective, fervent prayers that avail much, we must finish well. Praying though to the end is required for success. Prayer is a strange thing, it is easy to start, but often hard to finish. We see a need or we hear someone's plea and we want to pray. However, bringing our prayers to completion can be more difficult, it can be hard work.

People, by nature, respond to the world around them. Our response may take one of many forms, one of these is prayer. We have come to understand and believe that God responds to prayer, so when we are stirred by a stimulus and we respond by praying. For example, we have not had moisture in our area for several weeks, so people begin to pray, "Lord give us rain". Another example, we find out that a friend is sick, so we begin to pray, "Lord heal our friend".

If we choose to pray when we face problems this is a good thing. The difficulty comes after we begin to pray. Once we begin there are a wide range of hindrances fighting against us, trying to get us to stop praying. Hindrance's goal in the battle is to keep us from finishing God's assignment. The Father has called us to work and it is important that we begin, there are far too many times when people will not even start, but we must also work to finish that which is begun.

> *Jesus said to them, "My food is to do the will of Him who*
> *sent Me, and to finish His work.*
>
> JOHN 4:34 (NKJV)

Jesus completed His work; He was sent to purchase salvation for all who call Him Lord. His work of salvation is finished and complete. We do not add anything to it. The sacrifice of Jesus fully met every requirement God set for righteousness. In this way He finished the work He was sent to do. However, Jesus also continues to work; He has been and continues to make, intercession for us.

> *Who is he who condemns? It is Christ who died, and*
> *furthermore is also risen, who is even at the right hand of*
> *God, who also makes intercession for us.*
>
> ROMANS 8:34 (NKJV)

Therefore He is also able to save to the uttermost those
who come to God through Him, since He always lives to
make intercession for them.

HEBREWS 7:25 (NKJV)

Jesus was faithful to go to the cross and finish His work.
He also is faithful today, continuing to make intercession for
us. Unfortunately, most people are not nearly as faithful to finishing what they start. This is true in many aspects of life and
is also common in prayer. Often when people pray, they speak
out and then leave the prayer at that point; there is no follow
through of faith, no completion of what was started.

Prayer is by faith, no faith, no prayer and no answers. Until
there has been an application of faith, we do not have prayer.
And more importantly, until faith has been tested and found
to be victorious over doubt, fear, unbelief, and other sins and
hindrances, prayer is not complete.

If we are going to pray effective, powerful prayers, we must
finish the entire process. We need to begin to pray and then
stay in faith, never wavering until we complete the prayer.
Completion comes with the answer from God or when God
says the prayer is complete. There will be battles when doubt
tries to stop our prayer and we must stand firm in faith to the
finish. When fear comes to grab our heart with its icy grip, we
must keep our faith from growing cold. When doubt comes to
steal our faith, we must battle back using the Word of God, to
reject doubt and build faith.

And see, now I go bound in the spirit to Jerusalem, not
knowing the things that will happen to me there, except
that the Holy Spirit testifies in every city, saying that
chains and tribulations await me. But none of these things
move me; nor do I count my life dear to myself, so that

I may finish my race with joy, and the ministry which I received from the Lord Jesus, to testify to the gospel of the grace of God.

ACTS 20:22-24 (NKJV)

Prayer prayed to the finish, is praying and then standing in faith, never wavering, until the answer comes. This is what Paul did, he continued on to the finish. Paul's tells us he would not let anything keep him from finishing his race. We should have the same attitude in prayer, running the race to the end, to the successful end. We win the race, if we keep the faith. God is calling us to prayer. The question is, will we respond and pray? And once we begin will we fini...

I have fought the good fight, I have finished the race, I have kept the faith.

2 TIMOTHY 4:7 (NKJV)

Let us Pray!

DOGGED

When I was a boy I had a paper route and delivered afternoon papers to about 200 people. Part of my route went through a trailer court. At one of the trailers, there was a dog. It was a little dog who came out to bark at me every day. In addition to his bark this dog attempted to bite me. If I was slow in getting past this house, the dog would jump up and nip at my pants. This dog was very consistent, except when the weather was bad—the lady who owned the dog would not let him out in the snow—every day he attacked me with all of his might. He was amazing. He might have enjoyed seeing me leave the area, maybe he had a feeling of victory, I did leave his yard, but the next day here I came again. This went on everyday for several years, he never had the satisfaction of biting me or stopping my return, however, he was determined. His indomitable spirit would not be stopped.

We have a word in English for the actions of this dog, he was dogged. While this was not a trait that I appreciated in this little dog, it is an important trait for the man or woman of prayer. We are to be dogged in our prayers. This is not a suggestion that we should bark at God, most people do too much of that. We throw our criticisms and protests in His face, we moan and gripe and like that little dog we voice our displeasure. However, our situation is a little different from that of the dog, he was chasing a boy, and we are coming before the Almighty God.

Instead of complaining, our doggedness should be a tenacity and consistency in prayers. That little dog came after me every day. If we are to have effective prayers we must come before the throne of grace every day. Jesus told His disciples, and through them He tells us, that we should ask, seek, and knock. He explains these actions result in receiving, finding, and opening. And that is what we want in our prayers. To get this result we must be dogged, or persistent if you prefer. Read of this example of persistence.

> *And He said to them, "Which of you shall have a friend, and go to him at midnight and say to him, 'Friend, lend me three loaves; for a friend of mine has come to me on his journey, and I have nothing to set before him'; and he will answer from within and say, 'Do not trouble me; the door is now shut, and my children are with me in bed; I cannot rise and give to you'? I say to you, though he will not rise and give to him because he is his friend, yet because of his persistence he will rise and give him as many as he needs. So I say to you, ask, and it will be given to you; seek, and you will find; knock, and it will be opened to you. For everyone who asks receives, and he who seeks finds, and to him who knocks it will be opened.*
>
> LUKE 11:5-10 (NKJV)

This persistence is like the dogged nature of that little dog. The term dogged is not often used in association with prayer.

The more proper word is importunity. It is not a word commonly used today, but it is defined as an insistent or pressing demand. This is what Jesus was teaching and this should be our practice of prayer. We are to be importunate. Look at another teaching Jesus shared on this subject.

> *Then He spoke a parable to them, that men always ought to pray and not lose heart, saying: "There was in a certain city a judge who did not fear God nor regard man. Now there was a widow in that city; and she came to him, saying, 'Get justice for me from my adversary.' And he would not for a while; but afterward he said within himself, 'Though I do not fear God nor regard man, yet because this widow troubles me I will avenge her, lest by her continual coming she weary me.' "Then the Lord said, "Hear what the unjust judge said. And shall God not avenge His own elect who cry out day and night to Him, though He bears long with them? I tell you that He will avenge them speedily. Nevertheless, when the Son of Man comes, will He really find faith on the earth?"*
>
> LUKE 18:1-8 (NKJV)

Jesus explained that we are to be crying out day and night, we are to be dogged. He then asks a very important and revealing question. When the Son of Man comes, will He really find faith on the earth? Jesus speaking of prayer; asks about faith. It is easy to see that an important aspect of faith, when we pray, is importunity. We act in faith by crying out day and night. Even if God takes a long time to bring His answer, we are to doggedly continue in prayer. This is faith that we continue because we know He will answer.

Praying with importunity or doggedness is perseverance. Perseverance in prayer is to continue in prayer no mater what happens or how things seem to be going, good or bad. If we desire to pray and receive answers from God, we must be prepared to pray through to completion. This may take a great deal of effort and commitment. No matter if we have been praying for a few days, weeks, months, or years, today is not the day to stop. Effective, fervent prayer demands faith and sometimes faith is expressed by the act of doggedly continuing in prayer.

> *rejoicing in hope, patient in tribulation, continuing steadfastly in prayer;*
>
> ROMANS 12:12 (NKJV)

> *praying always with all prayer and supplication in the Spirit, being watchful to this end with all perseverance and supplication for all the saints--*
>
> EPHESIANS 6:18 (NKJV)

At times prayer can be frustrating, especially when answers seem a long time in coming. The Bible is filled with great stories of men and women of faith and their stories can be very helpful to us in learning about prayer and dealing with long waits. For example, Noah, Abraham, and Joseph had to deal with the pressure of a long wait. Day-after-day, year-after-year, they waited and then wait some more. It is amazing they were successful and amazing they fulfilled their dreams and destinies, but they did.

To wait for an answer from God is hard. These men's wait was so long, the wait was so hard to endure, yet wait they did. Don't you know people ridiculed Noah, "You are going to build an ark?" "It is going to rain?" Don't you know there was more than a few who wondered about Abraham having children at his age, "Your going to be the Father of many nations?" Don't you know his brothers questioned Joseph's dreams, when they were not just being angry with him? After being sold into slavery and then thrown into prison, still the dream did not come to pass. And then Joseph was forgotten in prison for two years.

> *Then it came to pass, at the end of two full years, that Pharaoh had a dream; and behold, he stood by the river.*
> GENESIS 41:1 (NKJV)

The list goes on and on, many other people of the Bible had long waits for answers and fulfillment of dreams. For most it looked impossible, they were, too old, too forgotten, too much in trouble, too hated, too everything except fulfilled and successful. Yet through it all, in every story listed here and many more, God brought them through. God at just the right time, in fulfillment of His purpose and plan, brought His answer. In each of our examples we see God's man or woman stand firm in faith.

> *Now faith is the substance of things hoped for, the evidence of things not seen. For by it the elders obtained a good testimony.*
> HEBREWS 11:1-2 (NKJV)

Further along in Hebrews we read of the faith of Abraham and Moses. We also read of the faith and exploits of other men and women of faith. Can you picture yourself in this list? What record is being written of your faith? What record is being written of the answers to your prayers?

> *By faith Abraham obeyed when he was called to go out to the place which he would receive as an inheritance. And he went out, not knowing where he was going. By faith he dwelt in the land of promise as in a foreign country, dwelling in tents with Isaac and Jacob, the heirs with him*

of the same promise; for he waited for the city which has foundations, whose builder and maker is God. By faith Sarah herself also received strength to conceive seed, and she bore a child when she was past the age, because she judged Him faithful who had promised. Therefore from one man, and him as good as dead, were born as many as the stars of the sky in multitude--innumerable as the sand which is by the seashore.

HEBREWS 11:8-12 (NKJV)

By faith Moses, when he became of age, refused to be called the son of Pharaoh's daughter, choosing rather to suffer affliction with the people of God than to enjoy the passing pleasures of sin, esteeming the reproach of Christ greater riches than the treasures in Egypt; for he looked to the reward. By faith he forsook Egypt, not fearing the wrath of the king; for he endured as seeing Him who is invisible. By faith he kept the Passover and the sprinkling of blood, lest he who destroyed the firstborn should touch them. By faith they passed through the Red Sea as by dry land, whereas the Egyptians, attempting to do so, were drowned.

HEBREWS 11:24-29 (NKJV)

All the heroes of the faith continue to give a good testimony. They are there to cheer us on to success. The new heroes of the faith are men and women of prayer. These heroes of the faith are committed to seeing God's Kingdom come on earth, as it is in Heaven. They pray to see the fulfillment of God's purpose and plan and they will see God complete and fulfill all He has begun to do.

However, even with these great examples, there are men and women around who continue to pray, but have not experienced the fulfillment of God's purpose and the answers of their prayers. They can say, "I have prayed, yet I am more like Joseph in the prison, than Joseph who ruled all the land of Egypt". They do not complain, but the questions it asked, why? What has happened? Where is the God who answers? So what is the problem and what must we do to have effective prayers? It is important for us not to blame God. The problem is not what is wrong with God, but what is wrong with man.

> *Then he took the mantle of Elijah that had fallen from him, and struck the water, and said, "Where is the Lord God of Elijah?" And when he also had struck the water, it was divided this way and that; and Elisha crossed over.*
> 2 KINGS 2:14 (NKJV)

Many years ago I heard a man preaching on verses from the Second Book of Kings. This preacher told us about a day in prayer when he was lamenting before God and he cried out, "Where is the God of Elijah?" and heard God reply, "Where are the Elijahs?" Beware, when we cry out, where is the God of the heroes of the faith? Or where is the God of the answers to prayer? God's reply may be somewhat like what God told this preacher, "Where are the men and women of faith"? He may reply, "Where are the men and women committed to answers in prayer?"

His reply is specific for you and your situation, it may be this or that, but in prayer His reply often will speak of our commitment or lack of commitment in prayer. Elisha picked up the Elijah's mantle and did all that Elijah had done and more. Why? Elisha was committed. No matter what people said or did, Elisha was committed to be there to see Elijah go to Heaven. He was committed.

Our call is to pray. If we are going to be successful in prayer, we must be committed. Remember that little dog that attacked me on my paper route, he would not stop no matter how much I kicked and yelled. Are you committed to answers in prayer with the tenacity of that dog? Elisha was committed. Jacob was committed, when he wrestled with God he said, "I will not let You go unless You bless me!" (See Genesis 32)

Many people pray, but are you willing to be like the Heroes of Faith, committed to continue no matter what comes? Far too often people are not dogged in prayer. Will you continue dogged to the end? Are you committed to seeing answers from God?

Let us Pray!

ARTICLE 24

DARKNESS

For a couple of years I worked as a computer operator for a computer firm in downtown Denver. The first two weeks I worked day shift and then I was transferred to swing shift, working from 4 pm to midnight. I drove to work in the afternoon before the afternoon rush hour and coming home there was very little traffic. It was wonderful not to have to fight the traffic and it was an easy drive most of the time. However, sometimes at night the trip could be difficult.

One night the drive started well, but when I got to the northern part of Denver it began to get foggy. The fog got thicker and thicker. My drive home was mostly on a good interstate road. It is well marked with two lanes going in my direction, but that night it got difficult to see the road. I kept slowing down so I could continue and try to be safe. Finally the fog got so bad all I could see was the lines between the lanes. This worked for a while, as long as I could see the next line I knew I was in my lane, but the fog got so thick I could not even see the next line.

Before I knew it, I had drifted away from my lane toward the edge of the road. It was only when I saw the solid white line that marked the edge of the road did I realize I was driving off the road. I was able to pull back on the road and continue. However, just then I saw a light coming straight at me. "I must be in the wrong lane or clear off the road", I thought and I stood on the breaks stopping the truck I was driving. Just as I came to a complete stop, I saw that the light was just the reflection of my headlights on the bottom of a coke can.

This was a frightening moment; I was stopped in the middle of an Interstate highway, and if there were other cars or trucks they could be going up to 55 miles per hour, which was the speed limit at that time. I got going again as quickly as I could. Moments later a truck went past me going very fast, but by then I was out of his way. A few miles down the road the fog began to lift and I could see to get home. It had been a scary drive, but God had protected me and kept me safe.

The first word in Christian life and in our prayer life is faith. All progress in life is by faith. Without faith we cannot please God, we are unable to live in His fullness, and unable to be effective in prayer. An important and often neglected factor of faith is darkness. In my story about the night of the fog please note there was more than one type of darkness. There was the darkness of night and the darkness from the fog.

In the Christian life and in prayer there are different types of darkness and we must learn to deal with them. It is important that we understand darkness, its various manifestations, and workings. A lack of understanding, affects the way we walk out our Christian life. This is especially important in prayer; effective prayer is by faith and unless we understand the working of darkness our faith will be weak and our prayers less than stellar.

One type of darkness is caused by sin. Sin is like a hood placed over our head causing a darkness that can be overwhelming and all but impenetrable. Like the fog in my story, the darkness of sin comes in varying degrees. This is not to say that any sin is less sinful than others, but as we walk in sin it can cover us with a heavier and heavier wrapping of darkness. Even with light fog, we cannot see clearly. Things around us are shrouded by this mist. Things are seen, but the details are not clear.

This lack of clarity is common when dealing with sin. We assume things that are not and imagine offence when none is given, we speak foolishly and we act in kind, we say and do things we should not. This is the fog of sin and it affects our life, both physical and spiritual. It causes a change in our thoughts, actions, beliefs, and of course of greatest importance, it limits the work of faith in our life. If we dabble in sin, it clouds our sight, we see, but not clearly. If we continue in sin, the fog grows thicker and denser and we fall into greater and deeper darkness.

> Behold, the Lord's hand is not shortened, That it cannot save; Nor His ear heavy, That it cannot hear. But your iniquities have separated you from your God; And your sins have hidden His face from you, So that He will not hear. For your hands are defiled with blood, And your fingers with iniquity; Your lips have spoken lies, Your tongue has muttered perversity
>
> ISAIAH 59:1-3 (NKJV)

> And have no fellowship with the unfruitful works of darkness, but rather expose them.
>
> EPHESIANS 5:11 (NKJV)

The darkness of sin keeps us from effective prayer. It separates us from God and closes the door on answers to our prayers. If we are going to have effective, fervent prayers that avail much, we cannot allow the unfruitful works of darkness to reside in our hearts. We must expose sin and its darkness, by confessing our sin and turning away from it.

> *But if we walk in the light as He is in the light, we have fellowship with one another, and the blood of Jesus Christ His Son cleanses us from all sin. If we say that we have no sin, we deceive ourselves, and the truth is not in us. If we confess our sins, He is faithful and just to forgive us our sins and to cleanse us from all unrighteousness.*
>
> 1 JOHN 1:7-9 (NKJV)

Most people are familiar with the workings of the darkness of sin. They have experienced its evil effects and twisted torment. However, fewer people are aware of the other types and effects of darkness. For instance, are you aware of the darkness of faith? We know that we must have faith for every aspect of the Christian life; this is especially true with prayer. Without faith there are no answers to prayer. Unfortunately, too often we think that we have faith. We think we are praying in faith, when what we are doing is resting on the visible and outward signs. No faith is used, because we can see what is happening and we go from sign to sign.

The nature of faith is dealing with darkness. If God was to show us everything He was doing and the results of what He was doing, we would not need faith; we would be walking by sight, not faith. We see this in many areas such as our salvation, which is by faith, not sight. We have to believe the promises of God and know by faith God has done and will do what He has promised. The just are saved by faith.

*Therefore, having been justified by faith, we have peace
with God through our Lord Jesus Christ, through whom
also we have access by faith into this grace in which we
stand, and rejoice in hope of the glory of God.*

ROMANS 5:1-2 (NKJV)

We are wonderfully saved, but this is not something we can
see in the natural today. We must believe by faith. There is
a darkness we must penetrate to be able to see by faith. John
Wesley described the penetration of the darkness by faith, as
his heart was strangely warmed. He was in darkness about salvation and then by the work of the Holy Spirit, he was able to
see, by faith, and was saved. He was able to bring many people
through the darkness to seeing, by faith, their salvation. I hope
the Holy Spirit has taken you through this darkness so you
can see, by faith, the salvation of God in your life!

This same type of darkness is found in prayer. At times
God will impress upon us a need for prayer. He calls us to pray
and believe Him for the needed answer. And then we must
deal with the darkness of faith. We must continue to believe
God's promises and pray, even when and especially when, we
see no progress or nearness of answer. He calls us to persevere
in prayer until the answer comes or He calls for us to stop our
labor. In faith we pray on, day-by-day, month-by-month and
may I even write it, year-by-year.

It is true that God sometimes gives signposts along the way.
The night I drove in the fog, it was wonderful to see the sign
telling how far it was to my home town. It was helpful to know
I was on the correct road and making progress toward my goal.
At times God does this in prayer. Look at Abraham, God vis-
ited and reconfirmed the goal of his prayers. God confirmed to
Abraham he would have a son.

Sometimes God does confirm and encourage our prayers with signpost along the way, but often He gives us a burden and expects us to continue by faith to the end, anything less than this is weakness of or lack of faith.

> "If there are encouraging signs to the natural eye our faith seems strong; but when, as with the story of the shipwreck in the book of Acts, neither sun nor stars appear for many days, we tend to abandon hope. It is not so much that a trail like this weakens our faith, it simply uncovers the true state of our hearts and shows us how weak our faith really is; that we are not truly walking by faith at all, but walking by sight". From *Pray in the Spirit* by Arthur Wallis

The darkness of faith demands an answer from you, are you walking by faith or by sight. When you pray do you walk by faith, seeking the answer, no matter the path, its roughness or length? Or must you have signs along the way to keep you from dropping the ball and ending your prayers? This is not easy, with no sign of progress, faith is hard. With no end in sight, faith is difficult to maintain. However, if we are going to pray and be effective for this generation and its needs, we must learn to and continue to pray in faith. If the Holy Spirit brings sign posts so be it, but if not, we must not quit until He says we are finished. Just a note here, the Holy Spirit does stop prayer. He stopped Jeremiah and He stopped Paul (Jer7:16 and Acts 16:6-10), so we can have great confidence He can and will stop us if need be. Since we can have confidence He will stop us, if He wants, we can have confidence to continue to pray, if He has not stopped us.

Dealing with darkness is not easy. The darkness of sin is a battle that only ends with graduation home to be with the

Lord. However, long though it may be, it is important that we do battle. We must resist sin and confess sin when we fail. Iniquity in our heart hinders and even stops the hearing of our prayers. We must work to be and continue to be right with God, anything less than this, results in failure in prayer.

If I regard iniquity in my heart, The Lord will not hear.

PSALM 66:18 (NKJV)

Dealing with darkness of faith is a battle as well. We must pray by faith and believe God for the answers. When the answer comes quickly the darkness issue is slight. When the answer is slow in coming or is delayed, darkness is an important issue. Far too often people have surrender to the darkness and ended their prayer. We must not surrender; the Holy Spirit will help us and support us if we will walk with Him. He helps us in our weakness and when the times are darkest. He can and will help us to walk through the darkness if we faint not.

Likewise the Spirit also helps in our weaknesses. For we do not know what we should pray for as we ought, but the Spirit Himself makes intercession for us with groanings which cannot be uttered.

ROMANS 8:26 (NKJV)

Now this is the confidence that we have in Him, that if we ask anything according to His will, He hears us. And if we know that He hears us, whatever we ask, we know that we have the petitions that we have asked of Him.

I JOHN 5:14-15 (NKJV)

Let us Pray!

THE IMPOSSIBLE MADE POSSIBLE

In Rocky Mountain National Park, a part of Colorado, the weather can change very rapidly. The sun can be out and very warm and then in a moment the clouds can blow in. With very little warning it can rain or even snow. When there is a storm the lightening strikes seem very close and the thunder so loud it shakes you and rumbles on and on through the canyons. If you are on a trail, especially a trail high on a mountain, when a storm springs up, you need to get to a safe place immediately. In some places there is nowhere to go except get down the trail quickly. The experienced hiker watches for storms and knows to move quickly when needed. If you are on a trail you might need to quicken your pace; double time or even triple time pace might be required.

Life is very much like Rocky Mountain National Park, things change very rapidly. Many things in life seem to remain about the same; everyone needs the basics for life and living, like food and shelter. Receiving these daily needs requires faith and prayer. We must believe God has, is, and will provide for our every need. He is our source and provision. As Jesus taught us, we should spend time with Him praying for our daily needs and for those around us. So we pray; "Our Father, give us this day our daily needs". This is the normal life of the believer and the life of prayer, the basics of faith and prayer, however there is more and things change.

There is so much to pray for and to pray about. Praying for all the situations that an individual faces requires a great deal of time, not to mention the needs of family, friends, and church. At times it seems this is all we can do; this takes our prayer time and our full effort. However, things change, there are storm clouds gathering and we must pick up the pace.

There is a need for men and women who will pray beyond the basics. There are people around us who need prayer, there are mission activities that need prayer, there are nations closed to the Gospel message that need prayer, and there are places in desperate need of revival that need prayer. All around us the situation of people daily grows graver. A generation is being swept into death and destruction; the storm clouds are growing and getting darker.

With these growing storm clouds there is an increasing need for prayer. Just like our climber who moves quickly down the trail to avoid a storm, we need to increase our prayers; to pick up the pace. The threat of the storms of life makes prayer imperative. All around us, in every country and nation there are people desperate for answers and help. They spread out before us like clouds and they are begging us to pick up the pace and pray.

This increase in prayer is not just putting in more time, but growing and maturing in prayer; in our efforts, skills, and faith. We must pick up our pace; not being satisfied with prayer as

THE IMPOSSIBLE MADE POSSIBLE

it has been, but move up to the place and pace the Holy Spirit has been preparing us for. The need is not for more of the same, but for effective, fervent prayers that avail much.

> ... *The effective, fervent prayer of a righteous man avails much.*
>
> JAMES 5:16 (NKJV)

Just like the man or woman on the trail moving along at a basic pace, when the clouds appear, they must move quicker. The clouds are appearing for us in prayer as well. The need has never been greater and the world is waiting. The world is asking; no it is begging, for you and me to pick up the pace and pray.

Let us Pray!

Men and women who will be faithful in prayer will pick up the pace. They see the need before us, people and nations in need of salvation, deliverance, protection, guidance, and provision and the answer for all of this begins with prayer. For those who have eyes to see what is happening the storm clouds are growing rapidly and getting very dark. In many ways things look hopeless, the need is too great and the situation too desperate. Many would say it is an impossible situation. However, our God is greater than all our needs. He has called for prayer and promises to answer. With His strong arm and powerful and wise strength, He can meet this need. He is calling for men and women to join with Him in the work by prayer and action. Too long we have tried to fix the problems we face by our own strength and wisdom, but it is not enough. Now we

145

must work by His guidance, empowerment, and grace and these come by prayer.

Unit four of this book is about making the impossible possible. God is able to do far beyond all that we think or imagine. He desires that we pray and not just little prayers, but prayers that bring situations that seem impossible into the possible and into reality. The articles of this book are intended to challenge you to think and dream big. The intent is to encourage you to pray for the seemingly impossible and make it, by God's answers, possible.

But Jesus looked at them and said to them, "With men this is impossible, but with God all things are possible."

MATTHEW 19:26 (NKJV)

But without faith it is impossible to please Him, for he who comes to God must believe that He is, and that He is a rewarder of those who diligently seek Him.

HEBREWS 11:6 (NKJV)

Now this is the confidence that we have in Him, that if we ask anything according to His will, He hears us. And if we know that He hears us, whatever we ask, we know that we have the petitions that we have asked of Him.

I JOHN 5:14-15 (NKJV)

A REQUEST

At this point we need to take time out. Before we go any further I would like to make a request. Most articles in *Voice of Thanksgiving* look at practices of effective prayer; things like making time for prayer, preparing our heart, changes to our life, and building our faith. We have looked at things as varied as removing hindrances to prayer, to becoming a craftsman of prayer. This article is a little different; I want to make a request.

Most of you reading this pray. Many of you have long years of experience praying and have long term prayer habits and projects. There are people, churches, ministries, and nations that fill your prayer time. Others of you are stepping into, or further into, a life of effective prayer. You have begun a journey that will take your prayers and intercessions to places all but unimaginable. I applaud your efforts and ask you, if you are a novice or experienced, to continue in your prayers. Your faithful, effective prayers are making a difference. However, today I make an additional request of you.

I am filled with concern for young people. I have worked with young people for many years as a teacher and administrator in public high schools. With this background I tend to notice young people. When I am places around Colorado or traveling overseas, my eye is caught by young people, noticing what they do and say. I have always enjoyed watching people, but young people take first place in my eye. Now I am more concerned than ever. In Colorado, throughout the USA, and around the world, young people are under attack.

It has always been a challenge for young people to deal with growing up. Growing up comes with many difficulties and problems. And this generation has more than its share to deal with. After World War I, many people called the generation of young people, those from many countries lost in the war, "the lost generation". I am concerned that the current generation of young people may be called the destroyed generation.

As difficult as it has been to deal with growing up, there has always been help available. In many societies families helped young people grow up and for centuries the keystone for success for young people has been Jesus Christ. Jesus lived, died, and rose from the dead, to deal with the needs of people, young and old alike. He brings life, abundant life.

> *The thief does not come except to steal, and to kill, and to destroy. I have come that they may have life, and that they may have it more abundantly.*
>
> JOHN 10:10 (NKJV)

Today the thief is attempting to destroy a generation of young people. So many of the safeguards for young people have been removed or cast away and the thief is having a field day with young people. Despair and death seem to reign supreme over the life of so many of this generation. Evil is ripening all around and having its harvest. For many young people the desire for living is being killed, the vitality of life is being stolen, and the fabric of life is being destroyed. This is the lot of millions of young people; however, there is another possibility.

I ask you to pray. We can make a difference for this generation. The so called "lost generation" marched off to war with marching bands and patriotic salutes and they died. However, we need not stand by and watch this generation march, to their destruction; we can pray. Our faithful, effective prayers can make a difference. It is by prayer that this generation will know abundant life in Christ Jesus. By prayer they will be seized from the grip of the thief and his destruction.

I know that many of you have a very full prayer life. You have many things that you pray for daily. I know that there are great and mighty things you labor daily for in prayer. However, I ask you to add to your prayer burden this generation of young people. I am asking that you would pray and fast for young people. Before us stands a massive field of people, ready for harvest. The question is how they will be harvested, will it be the thief who comes to steal, kill, and destroy or will they be gathered into the Kingdom of Heaven. Your prayers will make a difference.

Here is my request, pray for salvation and deliverance. Young people today are desperate for answers and for life. This struggle that they are in today is life and death, pray for them to hear the good news of the Gospel and choose life. Pray that there would be confusion in the thief's camp and his mission to destroy these young people would fail. Pray for hearts of young people to be opened and receptive to the Gospel message. Pray for ministries reaching out to young people. Pray for teachers and ministers to nurture and support these new converts as they move from death to life.

I ask you to pray for two groups of young people. First pray for the young people of your country. Each and every nation has difficult situations that young people face. Second, pray for the young people of another nation. The Holy Spirit is teaching us more and more about prayer and one of the key lessons is to pray for others. Let Him stretch you as you pray for the young people of another nation. There are young people on campuses of East Asia and young people in a school in Brazil. There are young people in a small town in Colorado and young people in cities and towns of Belarus. From Poland to Nepal there are young people who, as we sometimes say, "just chillin' on the corner" who may not know it, but they are waiting for harvesting. How will they be harvested? Will you pray?

> "Bear up the hands that hang down, by faith and prayer;
> support the tottering knees. Have you any days of fasting
> and prayer? Storm the throne of grace and persevere
> therein, and mercy will come down."
>
> John Wesley

Let us Pray!

PRAYING BIBLE VERSES

I n the previous article I made a request: the request, please pray for the young people of this generation. I hope that many of you responded, or will respond, to my appeal. This generation of young people is in need of a great deal of effectual, fervent prayer. They need answers from God for many things and in many areas; these answers will come through prayer. My point was, and is, that this generation needs to be snatched from the grip of the thief and gathered into the arms of Jesus who gives abundant life. If you responded to my request, or just continued to pray as you had been for young people, because it is a normal part of your prayer life, I say, thank you! Thank you for those who have and will turn from death to life!

> *The thief does not come except to steal, and to kill, and to destroy. I have come that they may have life, and that they may have it more abundantly.*
>
> JOHN 10:10 (NKJV)

In this article I would like to follow-up on this request. This is another opportunity for a teaching on prayer. There is a world of prayer that we need to explore and we should take opportunities like this to learn all we can. When explorers began dealing with the vastness of the North American continent, they had no idea of how massive the area was. Expedition after expedition explored the land and still there was more and more land to travel through. Prayer is like that. People have explored prayer for centuries, but there are many lessons still to learn and a great deal more to add to our understanding and practices of prayer.

One example of this is praying using verses of the Bible. In the Bible, John wrote about a world of prayer that few people have explored. Under the inspiration of the Holy Spirit he claims that when God hears us, we know we have what we ask for. That is powerful! For some people this is just too incredible to be true, so they dismiss it, losing the opportunity for their prayers. However, a few people have learned about the power promised in these verses. This power is available to all of us, not just a few.

> *Now this is the confidence that we have in Him, that if we*
> *ask anything according to His will, He hears us. And if*
> *we know that He hears us, whatever we ask, we know that*
> *we have the petitions that we have asked of Him.*
>
> 1 JOHN 5:14-15 (NKJV)

This is a very powerful statement on prayer. We can be confident that if we ask according to God's will, God will hear us and give us what we have asked for. "We know that we have the petitions that we have asked of Him". That is effectual prayer.

The key is asking according to God's will. If we know His will and ask accordingly, we will get answers. If we do not ask according to His will, we are not assured of answers. That is simple enough. It demands a man or woman willing to pray

and willing to know God's will. For the area you are praying, find out what He wants. One of the most effective ways
to know God's will is very simple; it is found in the Bible. For
centuries we have known God's will on a wide array of issues
and questions. It is recorded in the Bible.

> *All Scripture is given by inspiration of God, and is
> profitable for doctrine, for reproof, for correction, for
> instruction in righteousness, that the man of God may be
> complete, thoroughly equipped for every good work.*
>
> 2 TIMOTHY 3:16-17 (NKJV)

The Bible was given to equip us for work. This equipping is
how to live, how to love, how to minister, how to raise children,
how to work, how to play, and how to do every other aspect of
life. This includes how to be equipped for prayer! We need to
recognize the Bible as God's word on the subjects of life. The
Bible is His will for us for every area of our life.

> *Your word is a lamp to my feet and a light to my path.*
>
> PSALM 119:105 (NKJV)

> *For this reason we also thank God without ceasing,
> because when you received the word of God which you
> heard from us, you welcomed it not as the word of men,
> but as it is in truth, the word of God, which also effectively
> works in you who believe.*
>
> 1 THESSALONIANS 2:13 (NKJV)

A great way to know we are praying God's will is to pray using Bible verses and making them apart of our common practice. We know there is great power in praying God's will, so
why not pray God's will as recorded in the Bible. It is simple,
we need to find what He has said on the subject area of our

prayer and then pray those verses. For example we could pray these verses from the Psalms.

There they are in great fear, for God is with the generation of the righteous.

PSALM 14:5 (NKJV)

His descendants will be mighty on earth; the generation of the upright will be blessed.

PSALM 112:2 (NKJV)

This is God's will for this generation of young people. He wants them to be the generation of the righteous. He wants them to be the generation mighty on the earth; to be upright and blessed. It does not take much to be very excited about praying God's will in this case.

We might begin to pray something down the lines of this: "Father, I thank you that you care for these young people. Your love and your mercy fail not, for you never change. You continue to reach out to the lost and hurting of every generation and especially this generation. Father, cause this generation to seek You. Break through all the hindrances and barriers that have kept them from You. Cause this generation to fear Your name and come to the point of repentance, so they can be made righteous by the blood of Jesus. Father, I thank you for making this generation the generation of the righteous."

I asked that you also pray for people and ministries that work with young people and we can pray God's will for this request as well. We could begin with something like this: "Father, guide us in showing this generation Your strength and power. Let us not withhold telling of our praise of You and of Your strength and the wonderful works You have done". Here are some specific verses we can use.

Now also when I am old and grayheaded, O God, do not forsake me, Until I declare Your strength to this generation, Your power to everyone who is to come.

PSALM 71:18 (NKJV)

We will not hide them from their children, Telling to the generation to come the praises of the Lord, And His strength and His wonderful works that He has done.

PSALM 78:4 (NKJV)

One generation shall praise Your works to another, And shall declare Your mighty acts.

PSALM 145:4 (NKJV)

I hope you are excited about the possibilities for powerful, faith filled prayer for this generation of young people. We can pray that God's will to be done here on earth as it is in Heaven. We can confidently pray for this to be the generation of those who seek God.

This is Jacob, the generation of those who seek Him, Who seek Your face. Selah

PSALM 24:6 (NKJV)

Perhaps I could make my request yet again. Please pray for young people. Today I ask that you pray for this generation of young people, and that you practice praying Bible verses. I have given you a few verses for a start. Pick one or more of these or use one or more of your own. Pray God's will for the people of this generation.

Let us Pray!

LONG TERM PRAYER

As iron sharpens iron, So a man sharpens the countenance of his friend.

I have been blessed with good friends. They have remained friends with me in times both good and bad. They have continued to be friends even with a separation of long distance and through long gaps of irregular opportunities to see one another. These friends are true friends. They challenge me in my daily life and more importantly in my spiritual walk. They are good friends and close enough that they will not put up with negative things they see in me. I cannot roll around in the muck and mire of doubt and fear, they will not allow it. Hey, I told you they are good friends.

My good friends do more than just correct me when I am in the wrong. They walk with the Lord in ways that challenge me. We are close enough friends that I get to see how they live, even in tough or hard times. These friends are not perfect, I have seen times that they needed sharpening, and I have tried to return the favor. However, there are many areas where they challenge me and the way I walk through life. I hope they will challenge you today.

Several of these friends are gardeners. And more than just having a garden, they have long range plans for their garden and their whole yard. My wife and I grew plants in a garden for many years. We would prepare the ground, plant some seeds, and have a yield of a few vegetables. It was a garden, but it was not well planned, nor very fruitful. My friends have plans and their plans are far more detailed and challenging than anything my wife and I have done. In some cases I have watched their plans develop and grow for many years. Their plans have produced gardens and yards which have produced fruits and vegetables, enjoyment, and relaxation. The difference between my yard and theirs is their long term planning and hard work.

In prayer we see this same contrast. Most people are like my yard and me. We are willing and able to pray and we may pray in faith and see some results. Quick prayers and quick answers are okay (I enjoyed some tomatoes from my garden over the years). However, there is more; there is a lot more to prayer. There is a need today for men and women who will be more like my friends and their long term mentality. Long term prayer does not come to haphazard, short term thinking; it requires a commitment to staying the course, long term.

We need a mentality like my friends and their garden; we need long term prayer. There are examples of this in the Bible. The call for watchmen on the walls is not a short term or quick fix type of thing. God speaks of people who day and night, never give Him rest until answers come. We read that God has sought for someone to stand in the gap on behalf of the land. Standing duty like that is long term. Another example of this is the great zeal of Epaphras, who was always in prayer for the Colossians, Laodiceans, and those at Hierapolis. This takes time and great continuance of prayer. These examples are from a long time ago, but the need for long term prayer has not ended.

> *I have set watchmen on your walls, O Jerusalem; They shall never hold their peace day or night. You who make mention of the Lord, do not keep silent, And give Him no rest till He establishes And till He makes Jerusalem a praise in the earth.*
>
> ISAIAH 62:6-7 (NKJV)

> *The people of the land have used oppressions, committed robbery, and mistreated the poor and needy; and they wrongfully oppress the stranger. So I sought for a man among them who would make a wall, and stand in the gap before Me on behalf of the land, that I should not destroy it; but I found no one.*
>
> EZEKIEL 22:29-30 (NKJV)

> *Epaphras, who is one of you, a bondservant of Christ, greets you, always laboring fervently for you in prayers, that you may stand perfect and complete in all the will of God. For I bear him witness that he has a great zeal for you, and those who are in Laodicea, and those in Hierapolis.*
>
> COLOSSIANS 4:12-13 (NKJV)

For many of the needs we face today, long term prayer is the answer. God is looking for men and women who will pray. God's call for prayer includes seeking people willing to pray and receive answers quickly, but extends also to people willing to pray, even if it takes a long time to receive the answer.

The problem is few people will take the time and effort that is required to pray long term prayers. Far more than just saying the same prayer over and over, day-after-day, long term prayer is walking with God, by the guidance and help of the Holy Spirit, and coming to the place of abiding with God and knowing His will. The close relationship of abiding is required so we can, with His permission and encouragement, command His hand. For some prayers this may be difficult and it may take a while, even a lifetime to complete.

> *Thus says the Lord, The Holy One of Israel, and his Maker: "Ask Me of things to come concerning My sons; And concerning the work of My hands, you command Me".*
>
> ISAIAH 45:11 (NKJV)

Right up to the moment Jesus returns, there will be hearts that need to be prepared for receiving the Gospel. Until that last day, the governments of this world will need supplications, prayers, and intercessions. Even until the last trumpet calls, there will be a need for those who can pray and prepare the way for people and nations.

> *Therefore I exhort first of all that supplications, prayers, intercessions, and giving of thanks be made for all men, for kings and all who are in authority, that we may lead a quiet and peaceable life in all godliness and reverence. For this is good and acceptable in the sight of God our Savior, who desires all men to be saved and to come to the knowledge of the truth.*
>
> I TIMOTHY 2:1-4 (NKJV)

God is calling for men and women of prayer. He is looking for those who will serve Him, mankind, and nations, by praying, even long term, if needed. He is searching for men and women who will give their all for answers, even if this takes considerable time or super human effort. The Holy Spirit is willing and able to help us, if we will allow Him to work with us and train us to pray. Will you avail yourself to Him for long term prayer?

> *Likewise the Spirit also helps in our weaknesses. For we do not know what we should pray for as we ought, but the Spirit Himself makes intercession for us with groanings which cannot be uttered. Now He who searches the hearts knows what the mind of the Spirit is, because He makes intercession for the saints according to the will of God.*
>
> ROMANS 8:26-27 (NKJV)

> *He saw that there was no man, And wondered that there was no intercessor; Therefore His own arm brought salvation for Him; And His own righteousness, it sustained Him.*
>
> ISAIAH 59:16 (NKJV)

Let us Pray!

BIG CLAIMS AND PROMISES

One of the difficulties that men and women face when deal-ing with God is the enormity of His claims and prom-ises. He is just too big for us to understand. It is a little like the first white explorers when they came to Colorado. This re-gion was known for years as the Pike's Peak region. The name came from the mountain with this name and it was named for the leader of one of the early expeditions. The men of this expedition, coming from the east, saw the mountain far in the distance as they traveled across the plains. Not knowing how big the mountain was, they planned to camp at its base that night. It took three days to get to the base of the mountain. They made plans to climb the mountain the next day, but could complete only about two thirds of the climb to the top. This mountain is huge and finally they knew how big.

Dealing with things that are immense can be a problem. This is especially true concerning the things of God. His claims and promises are overwhelming and many people struggle to deal with the awesome possibilities. Look at the Jewish people, when they came out of slavery in Egypt. God promised to bless them and take them to the Promised Land. They faced the wrath of Pharaoh, the desert, lack of food and water, and the armies of other nations and although there were problems and delays, God brought them safely into the land. David faced Goliath, nevertheless he was confident with God's claims and promises and he defeated this giant and his army. Paul found, on the road to Damascus, that Jesus' claims and promises were powerful; they changed the heart of the persecutor, into its leading missionary apostle.

In these examples and many others, God is revealed to us, along with His enormous promises and claims. In our Christian and prayer life, we all must work our way through dealing with God's promises and claims. Just as the explorers got closer and were more and more impressed with Pike's Peak, as we draw near to God, we become more and more impressed with God's claims and promises.

The Bible is filled with these claims and promises. More important than the number of claims and promises, is their magnitude. He does not claim He can give you "get by" life, He claims that you can have life and more abundantly. He is the God of the awesome claims and the enormous promises.

> *The thief does not come except to steal, and to kill, and to destroy. I have come that they may have life, and that they may have it more abundantly.*
>
> JOHN 10:10 (NKJV)

> *Therefore I say to you, whatever things you ask when you pray, believe that you receive them, and you will have them.*
>
> MARK 11:24 (NKJV)

Read the verse from Mark again. We need to appreciate what the Bible is saying here. This will help us understand how big God is and how big His claims and promises are. Study some of the key words, for instance, the word, ask, in this verse. In the Greek this word means; to ask, beg, call for, crave, desire, or require. In this verse we also have the word "pisteuo", which is translated, believe and means, to have faith. There is the phrase, "will have them", which comes from the Greek word "lambano", to take or to get hold of. This verse claims, we can ask or require in prayer, by faith, and take hold of the things we need. This is a great promise, but there is more. There is the meaning of one other word that should be noted, it is the Greek word "hosos". This word means, as much as, as great as, or as long as. Jesus said; "Whatever (hosos) things you need". We can ask for whatever we need? Yes!

The man or woman who longs for answers to prayer, who longs for a full and effective prayer life, will work to accept and embrace the awesome claims and enormous promises. The great men and women of prayer, our examples and mentors in faith and prayer, climbed part way up this mountain. They accepted the claims and promises of God as true; they prayed and got answers. However, notice that I said they climbed part way up this mountain; they did not take in all of this claim and promise. The greatest Christian of faith and prayer has never embraced all of what God is claiming and promising. There is much more for us to comprehend, utilize, apprehend, and apply to our life and prayers.

Now is the time for us to seek to appropriate and apply all of God's claims and promises. Even this is an enormous thought, but it is one that is needed for the world and its problems today. In these the last days before the return of Christ, the people of the world need to hear the Gospel. The business of taking the Gospel to souls from every nation, in this generation, is far too enormous for mission organizations and churches to complete without effective, powerful prayer. We must have men and women of prayer, those who will pray in faith, believing the awesome claims and enormous promises of God are true and available to meeting our needs. We need you (and me) to believe and pray and then act on God's answers!

Father, please bring our hearts to the place where we long to receive all your claims and promises. Change our hearts so we do not limit what you have said, nor limit what you do. Do not let us be satisfied with normal everyday life, but draw us up the mountain of acceptance of Your awesome claims and enormous promises as true and for us today. Father, cause us to seek after Your high calling; that is, that we would pray expecting that we would receive whatever we need in prayer.

Let us Pray!

IMPOSSIBLE

I n the Bible there are scores of events recorded and many of these, seen before the event, seemed to be impossible. With our scientific minds and confident assurance that we understand what is happening around us, we must be careful or we will discount these events. Modern man claims a very strong sense of what is possible and what is impossible. Modern, sophisticated man views the story of Elijah with disdain, but he did pray down fire. The sophisticate looks for "more plausible" explanations to the story of Moses and the Jewish people. However, the Jews did successfully cross the Red Sea, while Pharaoh and his army failed. Modern man wants to explain things as just a fairy-tale, but Jesus did turned water into wine.

God doing the seemingly impossible is a central theme of the Bible and Christian life. The most important example is justification, which is by faith. A key component of justification is the incarnation of Jesus. The incarnation seems impossible, God became man, but this is the essential to the justification of man. While it may be difficult for us to understand, it is a fact and we can and must rest our faith on this seemingly impossible fact.

Much of our industrial and technological might is built on our dealing with the seemingly impossible. Both accepting the impossible and rejecting the seemingly impossible has served us well. The alchemist of the Middle Age tried to change base metals into gold, he failed. He could not make a transition from one element to another. However, out of these failures other men realized that substances did not change; the basic characteristics of materials do not change. In consistent conditions, materials will act the same every time. This was an important discovery because it makes modern industry and technology possible.

Until we knew that things will act the same all the time, we could not count on using them. Now an engineer can test a wing for an airplane on a computer even before the wing is built because he knows carbon fibers prepared to a set of specifications, will always act within those specifications. A compound of chemicals combined in a specific formula always gives aspirin, just as it did so many years ago when first discovered. A specific type of plastic excreted from a machine, will always hold our coffee warm and safe, our only fear is clumsiness, not that the plastic will suddenly change and the hot coffee will flow from the container.

By contrast refusing to accept the seemingly impossible has also fueled the rush of progress in industry and technology. The great inventions have come from men and women refusing to listen when they were told, "It is impossible." Everyone saying, "It is impossible," set the Wright brothers soaring above the chorus of naysayers. "It is impossible," caused Bill Gates to bite the apple and create the personal computer. "It is impossible," brought to light the stubbornness of Thomas Edison, so that even after thousands of failures, he brought safe illumination to the world. The list goes on and on. Time-after-time people have chosen to go against the commonly held view of what is impossible and found a way to make the seemingly impossible, possible. For some people hearing, "It is impossible", sets them off in a frantic search to make it happen.

The impossible and the seemingly impossible are foundational to prayer as well. Without the impossible, prayer is nothing more than mindless chanting, like that of pagan religions. For the Christian, the impossible makes prayer not just a duty or ritual, but the source of life and power. The most important impossible is centered not on the consistency of metals and chemicals, but on God Himself. It is impossible for Him to change, He is never changing always consistent.

"For I am the Lord, I do not change;

MALACHI 3:6 (NKJV)

If He were fickle, changing on every whim, we would never pray. It would be senseless to pray. Even if He listened and spoke, it would be of no value, for the yes, of today, could be the no, of tomorrow. Without the "impossible for Him to change" nature, prayer is a wasted effort. Just as the chemist must know that the elements in aspirin never change, so we must know that God does not change. He is and must be the same yesterday, today and forever.

Jesus Christ is the same yesterday, today, and forever.

HEBREWS 13:8 (NKJV)

Every good gift and every perfect gift is from above, and comes down from the Father of lights, with whom there is no variation or shadow of turning.

JAMES 1:17 (NKJV)

But there must be more to the impossible in prayer; it is not enough for God just to not change. Even the god of the Philistines in the Old Testament, Dagon never changed, he was a hunk of stone carved like half a fish. He just sat where ever they put him. God is different, He listens to our prayers. The prayers to Dagon dropped to the floor and were not answered. God hearing and answering is required for effective prayer and God promises to listen and answer. It seems impossible, but it is true. It is impossible for our Father to lie and He promises to listen to and answer our prayers.

> 'Call to Me, and I will answer you, and show you great and mighty things, which you do not know.'
>
> JEREMIAH 33:3 (NKJV)

> Now this is the confidence that we have in Him, that if we ask anything according to His will, He hears us. And if we know that He hears us, whatever we ask, we know that we have the petitions that we have asked of Him.
>
> I JOHN 5:14-15 (NKJV)

The nature of God is not changing. He does what He says He will do. He promises to listen and speak to us and He cannot lie. Being faithful to His word, claim, and promise is a key feature of His nature. It is a very positive impossible. It is impossible for God to not be whom and what He is. This makes effective prayer possible and valuable.

> Thus God, determining to show more abundantly to the heirs of promise the immutability of His counsel, confirmed it by an oath, that by two immutable things, in which it is impossible for God to lie, we might have strong

consolation, who have fled for refuge to lay hold of the hope set before us.

The seemingly impossible is important in prayer as well. We are sons and daughters of the God who does things even when they seem impossible. The Bible is filled with God doing the seemingly impossible. From stopping and starting rainstorms to twilight walks on lakes, He is not restricted by the seemingly impossible. From flowing fountains of oil filling pots and pans, to fine wine from water for weddings, He is not hindered by what most people see as impossible. From pulling down city walls, to opening prison gates, He is not waylaid by the seemingly impossible. God is not limited by situations and problems. He has chosen to respond to prayer and He as made nothing impossible when He is asked.

But He said, "The things which are impossible with men are possible with God."

LUKE 18:27 (NKJV)

Most problems in prayer come from people's trouble in dealing with the impossible. It is easy to come to the place where we doubt the impossible, believing that God changes, doesn't listen, or is not able to work for us. This brings us to a place where we believe that the impossible is impossible. This limits answers to prayers.

Men and women are comfortable questioning God and His nature, yet hold fast to the unyielding nature of what they believe cannot be. This is devastating to prayer. It is impossible to pray, with faith, with a false view of God and a false view of what He can and cannot do. Too often we get these reversed; we think it is possible for God to change and be fickle (most often we are blaming Him for our fickleness). At the same time we become convinced that there are things that cannot be changed; situation and conditions are more real, lasting, and unchangeable. No matter how long or how well we pray, with this reversal of thinking, we pray in doubt and unbelief. There cannot be faith when we cannot trust God. There cannot be faith when we don't believe He can do the seemingly impossible.

Check your prayer life; examine it closely. Where do you stand on the impossible and the seemingly impossible? If these have become twisted in any way, you need to recognize this situation and make changes. We must comprehend and put into practice, understanding of God as revealed in the Bible. We must have faith and pray according to the revelation that God can and does change the seemingly impossible. We must hold fast to our faith, proclaiming God can, has done, and will do the seemingly impossible, in response to our prayers.

Let us Pray!

ANSWERS TO THE SEEMINGLY IMPOSSIBLE

The word, impossible, controls much of a person's life. When he believes something is impossible it is very difficult to change his mind. We have such confidence in the impossible we seldom will even try something we have deemed to be impossible. In America there is an expression, "You can't teach and old dog new tricks." Since it is deemed by most people that teaching an old dog to do new tricks is impossible, few people will even try. For all they know old dogs may learn faster or better compared to young dogs, but they will not try because they believe it is impossible.

There are few things as powerful as the impossible. Once we declare something impossible it seems as though there is no going back. This has been true for most of the people of every generation, but not for everyone. Some people go against this trend, they do not believe impossible always means impossible. Something that people have declared to be impossible is just a call to them to try to do the seemingly impossible. History records many who have tried new things and found out that it was not impossible. Many of these people would not take no for an answer. They just continued to try to make changes until they found a way that worked.

Others have overcome the limitations of the impossible by developing an understanding of the nature and abilities of God. They have walked in faith and experienced God's power. They have found that He is not limited by what people declare possible or impossible. They know the seemingly impossible is possible for God. Many of these people are unknown to most of the world, others are well know, such as those recorded in the Bible, but what they all have in common, is reaching out to God in faith and seeing Him move powerfully on their behalf. These are heroes of the faith and they have seen God do the seemingly impossible.

> *Now to Him who is able to do exceedingly abundantly above all that we ask or think, according to the power that works in us,*
>
> EPHESIANS 3:20 (NKJV)

Acting beyond all we ask or think, is God doing the seemingly impossible. We are encouraged to ask, knowing that if we believe, by faith, God will answer. God is not limited by our narrow thinking and He goes well beyond accepted wisdom. He is willing, able, and He often does do what looks impossible to most people. He has declared that men and women of faith will see the seemingly impossible done. The heroes of the faith have joined with God in getting great and wonderful things done and we can join with Him as well.

Few people experience the seemingly impossible made possible, why are there so few? There are many factors to this question. We will just touch on a few points here, the scope of this article does not allow for an in-depth study of the question. Here we will look briefly at our preparation. Are we primed to experience the power of God making the seemingly impossible into the possible?

First, we must authorize God to work. This may seem strange to some, but God does not force Himself on us. He does not even force blessings on us. We ask Him to come into our life and we give Him authority to work. We must say yes and mean yes, when we actually invite him in, we are opening the door for God. Many people talk about God moving in their life, but for various reasons they really mean, no, do not come in. Dealing with God can be overwhelming and it sometimes seems easier to say no to God. A question for us to ponder, a question we must explore with the Holy Spirit's help, have we authorized God to work in our life.

Second, we must align our life, thoughts, and actions with Gods will. When we pray we need to pray God's will, but we need to also bring into line every aspect of our life with God's plans and directions. There is a broad way, traveled by the world, but this is neither God's way, nor the best way. Travel on God's way is by faith and it is in alignment with His word, the Bible.

> And an highway shall be there, and a way, and it shall
> be called The way of holiness; the unclean shall not
> pass over it; but it shall be for those: the wayfaring men,
> though fools, shall not err therein. No lion shall be there,
> nor any ravenous beast shall go up thereon, it shall not
> be found there; but the redeemed shall walk there: And
> the ransomed of the Lord shall return, and come to Zion
> with songs and everlasting joy upon their heads: they shall

obtain joy and gladness, and sorrow and sighing shall flee
away.

ISAIAH 35:8-10 (KJV)

Success in prayer comes from close association with God. Jesus made provision for us so we can walk God's way but, we must choose to go His way. In the first book of Samuel, we read about a woman of prayer and her powerful prayer. Her life was miserable and the only thing that could fix the problem was a son. Hannah was desperate for a son, but instead of complaining, she prayed and God heard her prayer. When she prayed, she declared that if given a son she would dedicate him to God. God gave Hannah a son (Samuel).

And she was in bitterness of soul, and prayed to the Lord
and wept in anguish. Then she made a vow and said, "O
Lord of hosts, if You will indeed look on the affliction of
Your maidservant and remember me, and not forget Your
maidservant, but will give Your maidservant a male child,
then I will give him to the Lord all the days of his life, and
no razor shall come upon his head."

I SAMUEL 1:10-11 (NKJV)

So it came to pass in the process of time that Hannah
conceived and bore a son, and called his name Samuel,
saying, "Because I have asked for him from the Lord."

I SAMUEL 1:20 (NKJV)

A prayer such as, "God I need answers to the impossible mess of my finances", is a reasonable request. To anticipate Him moving on our behalf is a reasonable expectation, but we need to check and see if we are associated with Him and His purposes. We should check; are our finances dedicated to Him and His Kingdom or for our personal use? God is willing and able to supply for our needs, even beyond our immediate needs.

He longs to bless us so we can be a blessing. We need to check, is our request to feed our lusts, to pad our life so we do not have to trust God, or so we can bless? Is my desire to seek first His kingdom, even in my finances? If I want to pray powerful prayers that avail much, I should be asking, what is God doing in my generation, my fellowship, and my life and have I dedicated my life to be apart of what He is doing? Am I seeking first His kingdom?

Third, we need to check and see if we are under authority. Who rules in your life, God, self, flesh…? The man under authority understands that being under God's authority is the place of receiving from Him and the place of His power. The Centurion from Capernaum understood authority; he knew that just as he ruled by his authority, so also Jesus could heal because He had authority over sickness and disease.

> *For I also am a man under authority, having soldiers under me. And I say to this one, 'Go,' and he goes; and to another, 'Come,' and he comes; and to my servant, 'Do this,' and he does it." When Jesus heard it, He marveled, and said to those who followed, "Assuredly, I say to you, I have not found such great faith, not even in Israel!*
>
> MATTHEW 8:5-13 (NKJV)

We long for the blessing of being under God's authority, but we do not follow through. We claim to be under authority, and then do our own thing. We say Jesus is Lord, but in the next breath we deny His Lordship over our sickness, problem, or need. We negate our faith and stop His work, because we are not really under authority. We do our own thing, trying to rule our own life. We long for His help and support, but want it our way. Is it any wonder we do not receive answers to our prayers. We make His answers to the seemingly impossible, impossible.

> Set a guard, O Lord, over my mouth; Keep watch over the
> door of my lips. Do not incline my heart to any evil thing,
> To practice wicked works With men who work iniquity;
> And do not let me eat of their delicacies.
>
> PSALM 141:3-4 (NKJV)

How did you check out, have you given authority to God, are you associated with Him, and under His authority? If your answer is no, then seek help from the Holy Spirit and make changes. If your answer is yes, then you are in a good place to see God do great things in your life. You can anticipate and expect answers to your prayers. You can expect to see God change the seemingly impossible into the possible.

Let us Pray!

ARTICLE 31

THE NORMAL CHRISTIAN LIFE

I have been blessed to go on many mission trips. Year-after-year God has provided me with opportunities and means of going, so I can experience His power and workings. Even from the very first trip, He made it clear that He would not be limited to what I thought He could or could not do. He would not be limited by money, plans, timing, airlines, or expectations.

For example, on the first mission trip, which I expected to go to South America, but went to Europe instead, God demonstrated His unlimited nature and power. One of the stops on this trip was in Innsbruck, Austria and over dinner I discovered that my host had planned to work with a team witnessing to people at the Olympic Center. This is where the Olympic ice events were held during the 1964 Winter Olympics and where, that night, there was a presentation of the musical, *Jesus Christ Superstar.*

The plan was to be outside the center when the musical ended and pass out tracts and talk to people. Over dinner my host stated that he had planned for me to come with the team. I was shocked, I did not speak very much German, and I was convinced there was nothing I could do. However, I did not want to wreck the plans or limit the others faith, so I said I would love to go.

All the members of the team meet before going to the Olympic Center and we prayed. I joined in the prayer time and thought this was my main role for the night. When we got to the Olympic Center all the members of the team were given witnessing tracts to give to the people. It was decided that I could give out tracts and a smile; if I needed more than this, I could ask others on the team for help. The evening was a success, the team got to talk to many people and share about salvation through Christ Jesus.

After the crowd left the area, we packed up and decided we wanted to get something to eat and talked about the events of the evening. Near by was a McDonald's, and as it was fast and cheap, this is where we went. While standing in line to order, we noticed that the people coming in were all wearing jackets from the show, *Jesus Christ Superstar*. Most of the cast had come to McDonald's for a bite to eat after the show.

The cast, as we found out, was from New York and most of them were Americans. Suddenly there was an opportunity to talk to these young people and share the Gospel. Turning to the man in line behind me I asked him, "Who are you?" Without missing a beat he said, "I am Jesus Christ." I then ask him, "Do you know Him?" For the next few minutes, members of the team, who spoke English and I got to talk with these cast members and share about the true message of the musical, Jesus Christ, the real Superstar!

God had taken the impossible; I could not talk to Austrians about my faith because of limitations in my ability to speak German, and made sharing the Gospel possible. If I had acted on the impossible situation, as I saw it, and chosen not to go with the team, I would have missed the opportunity to share the Gospel and to see God do the seemingly impossible.

Watching God do the seemingly impossible is very exciting. This should be a regular part of our life. It should be a regular part of our prayer life. This requires praying in faith.

Praying faith filled prayers should be the normal life of all Christians. Faith is not something just for a few select men and women, it is for all Christians. It is for you and me. The life we live now should be a life of faith. The work we do now should be founded on, empowered by, and directed by faith. The prayers we pray should receive extraordinary answers by faith. This is how we should live as Christians. There is no division in the Christian world, no second class citizens; we are Christians, purchased to an abundant life, by the work of Jesus Christ. His infilling of life and faith is perfect for meeting the requirements of God and meeting our every need, now and forever.

> *And having been perfected, He became the author of eternal salvation to all who obey Him,*
>
> HEBREWS 5:9 (NKJV)

> *looking unto Jesus, the author and finisher of our faith, who for the joy that was set before Him endured the cross, despising the shame, and has sat down at the right hand of the throne of God.*
>
> HEBREWS 12:2 (NKJV)

Young Christians do great things. Their witness of the Gospel can be and often is very powerful. They make great members of a witnessing team. The promises of God are so fresh and real to them that they just naturally stand confident in Him. They remember that they were in an impossible situation and God took them out of that situation and brought them into His Kingdom. Their thinking is simple, if God can do the impossible for me, why should we not expect Him to do it again now? With this mindset they are bold.

Unfortunately, it is common for people to lose this confidence in God. They learn to limit God, His willingness and ability. The impossible is impossible. They learn to not live the normal Christian life (*The Normal Christian Life* is the title of a book by Watchman Nee. It is a study on living our life in the fullness of Christ, claiming this should be the normal life for all Christians). The true normal Christian life sees God doing the seemingly impossible regularly.

If we are going to do what God has called us to do, reaching our generation with the Gospel and helping people enjoy the abundant life Jesus promised, we must return to the normal Christian life. We must walk in God's supernatural abilities and power and pray; anything less will leave us overwhelmed by the impossible situation of self, men, and nations. The limitless power of God is at our disposal. He promises to listen if we will pray and so we must pray. Our prayers must go beyond the limits of the possible and trust in His ability and willingness to do the seemingly impossible.

Faith makes doing the seemingly impossible, possible. We can and should be asking for His power and expecting Him to get the seemingly unattainable, to do the out of the question, and accomplish the unachievable. God is in the "doing the impossible business" and He wants us to join Him as full partners in the firm. Our job is to ask. We must ask as He directs and orders; we must ask in faith, but ask we must.

If we will ask God, in faith for the things He wants us to do, we can have His unlimited power in prayer. No matter what we face, problems, conflicts, hindrances, or anything else, we can pray, we must pray, and we must believe that God can and will make the seemingly impossible, possible. We can expect our limitless Father to answer our prayers with His unlimited, situation changing power. The world is waiting; they are wondering, will we pray?

> 'Call to Me, and I will answer you, and show you great and mighty things, which you do not know.'
>
> JEREMIAH 33:3 (NKJV)

> Now to Him who is able to do exceedingly abundantly above all that we ask or think, according to the power that works in us,
>
> EPHESIANS 3:20 (NKJV)

> But without faith it is impossible to please Him, for he who comes to God must believe that He is, and that He is a rewarder of those who diligently seek Him.
>
> HEBREWS 11:6 (NKJV)

> Now this is the confidence that we have in Him, that if we ask anything according to His will, He hears us. And if we know that He hears us, whatever we ask, we know that we have the petitions that we have asked of Him.
>
> I JOHN 5:14-15 (NKJV)

Let us Pray!

MISSED OPPORTUNITY

It was an opportunity and I missed it. My time in the US Air Force was great; I met some great people and saw Europe for the first time. It also was frustrating because there were things I missed. One of the things I missed was seeing friends and family. This was especially true with not getting to spend time with my Grandpa. For years he and I had been very close. I thought he was wonderful; he could build things, he was a great fisherman, and I believed he could do anything. So it was hard not getting to see my Grandpa very often during those years.

One of the few times during this period I saw Grandpa, when I was home on leave; we got to spend time without the rest of the family. We just talked and enjoyed being together. As we talked I had an opportunity to share the Gospel message. There was a moment in our conversation when I could have asked him about his relationship with the Lord, but I did not ask. I missed the opportunity and for a long time this missed opportunity weighed heavy on me. It turned out to be the last time I saw my Grandpa alive here on earth.

One day after I got out of the Air Force, I was talking to my bother Bill and we began to talk about Grandpa. We talked of some of the wonderful times when we had been fishing and the fun we had. I expressed a little of my frustration that I had not talked to Grandpa about his faith. And Bill began to talk about a time he had alone with Grandpa just a few weeks after I had gone back to military duty. The question of salvation came up. Bill had shared the Gospel and Grandpa had responded, making Jesus Lord of his life. I was so relieved. It was wonderful to know that God had overcome my missed opportunity and helped my Grandpa. God was also gracious to let me know He had taken care of the missed opportunity another way.

How about you, have you missed opportunities? Most everyone has, but hopefully it was not something as important as sharing the Gospel. But most of us know the feeling all to well, there is an opportunity to speak, to act, to share, to help, to love, to care, or to do something for someone else and we have missed the opportunity. Opportunities are times when the moment is right and the Holy Spirit will nudge us and encourage us to speak or act. Sometimes we respond well, but other times we miss the boat. Later we have that sinking feeling and a realization that we have missed a chance. Paul understood opportunities and he did not want to miss them or let anything hinder him from making the most of them.

> For a great and effective door has opened to me, and there are many adversaries.
>
> I CORINTHIANS 16:9 (NKJV)

> praying always with all prayer and supplication in the Spirit, being watchful to this end with all perseverance and supplication for all the saints-- and for me, that utterance may be given to me, that I may open my mouth boldly to

*make known the mystery of the gospel, for which I am an
ambassador in chains; that in it I may speak boldly, as I
ought to speak.*

EPHESIANS 6:18-20 (NKJV)

There is a wide variety of opportunities and we all get chances to be faithful and respond. It is so important that we practice taking opportunities and making the most of them. Taking opportunities brings with it a risk factor. You could have a bad experience or things might not go as you want. However, an opening is presented to you because God believes you are ready and able to respond. We are just messengers and laborers, it is His message, and His working that makes the difference. A new creation in Christ Jesus can be bold; we are born new in Christ and His power. If we cannot take risks, then it would be good to evaluate if we are truly crucified with Christ. The question should be asked, am I a new creation in Christ Jesus or just a religious Christian protecting my image and feelings?

*I have been crucified with Christ; it is no longer I who live,
but Christ lives in me; and the life which I now live in the
flesh I live by faith in the Son of God, who loved me and
gave Himself for me.*

GALATIANS 2:20 (NKJV)

For to me, to live is Christ, and to die is gain.

PHILIPPIANS 1:21 (NKJV)

There is another realm of opportunities and these are also ones we do not want to miss. We have opportunities in prayer. We have been called to pray and we believe our prayers make a difference. We know that God listens and responds to prayer, so we should expect that we will be given opportunities to pray. Some of these opportunities will be special and specific;

just like the opportunities we see in our daily life, for example when we are confronted with an opportunity, such as sharing the Gospel. The opportunity is special, of inestimable importance, and specific, it is an appointed time. We face opportunities in prayer that are just as special and specific. The question, just like in all opportunities, how will we respond?

Far too often we face missed opportunities in prayer. There are one hundred and one excuses why we missed the opportunity; I missed the opportunity in prayer, because I wasn't there to get the assignment. I missed because I do not have regular prayer times. I missed because I do not go to regular prayer meetings. I missed because I did not pray that day.

Even if we are praying we can miss. I missed the opportunity in prayer because I wasn't listening. I did not listen because I did all the talking that day. I did not listen because I just complain, not praying. I did not listen because I have never learned to hear the voice of the Lord. I did not listen because I do not believe that God speaks today.

There are additional possibilities for missed opportunities. I missed the opportunity in prayer because I was not ready to hear or respond. I missed the opportunity because I was caught up in fear. I did not pray because I was so angry I could not pray. I did not pray because I would not forgive. I missed the opportunity because I held onto a sin. I missed because I let hindrances keep me from prayer or keep me from the opportunity.

I missed the opportunity because I did not believe God would speak to me. I did not believe God would use me to pray. I did not believe God would give me an assignment in prayer. I did not believe that He would trust me. I did not believe that God would answer my prayers.

The list goes on and on. The bottom line is men and women faithful in prayer will have opportunities to pray. Some opportunities will be simple things others will be great things, but the question remains, what we will do with the opportunity. The faithful in prayer believe God. They know He has made us a new creation, a new person. They know we should and can pray. They know this new person has been given an opportunity to pray in faith, praying effective, fervent prayers that avail much. So faithful person, will you take the opportunities?

Let us Pray!

PRAYER FOR SALVATION

Problems and disasters are all around; a quick look at a news report confirms that difficulties are popping up everywhere. The problems are so widespread and so bad it makes you wonder what to do.

The Bible reveals that there would be times like these and there is only one answer, Jesus Christ. Today is a great time for you to get to know Him. Read these verses from the letter to the Romans. If you believe in your heart as these verse say, you can be saved. Read the verse and then pray the prayer. Pray with sincerity and trusting God and be born again.

> *that if you confess with your mouth the Lord Jesus and*
> *believe in your heart that God has raised Him from the*
> *dead, you will be saved. For with the heart one believes*
> *unto righteousness, and with the mouth confession is*
> *made unto salvation.*
>
> ROMANS 10:9-10 (NKJV)

Dear God in Heaven, I recognize that I am a sinner, and I need help. I come to you in the name of Jesus to receive salvation and eternal life. I believe that Jesus is your Son. I believe that He died on the cross for my sins and that you raised Him from the dead. I receive Jesus now into my heart and make Him the Lord of my life. Jesus come into my heart, I welcome you as my Lord and Savior. Father, I believe Your Word says, that I am now saved. I confess with my mouth that I am saved and born again. I am now a child of God.

Congratulations you are now part of the body of Christ!

NOW WHAT SHOULD YOU DO?

Tell someone of your decision (you could email me at dave@voiceofthanksgiving.com)

Get a Bible and read it

Find a Christian church that believes the Bible, be an active and faithful participant at meetings

Get baptized

VOICE OF THANKSGIVING

The *Voice of Thanksgiving* is a newsletter calling men and women to effective prayer. *Voice of Thanksgiving* is published in a weekly version in English and monthly versions, in German and Polish. Articles from the newsletter and much more can be seen at the *Voice of Thanksgiving* website. This website contains an archive of past issues, a prayer blog, and useful information and resources on prayer, intercession, and victorious Christian living. The *Voice of Thanksgiving* website can be seen at: http://voiceofthanksgiving.com

Prayer: A Force that Causes Change – A Call to Prayer
Prayer: A Force that Causes Change – A Life of Prayer
Prayer: A Force that Causes Change – Faithful in Prayer
Copies of these books are available at:
http://voiceofthanksgiving.com/Book/Book.htm

To receive *Voice of Thanksgiving* weekly by email, send an e-mail with word JOIN in the subject line to:
david@voiceofthanksgiving.com